Milton Henry Stine

A Winter Jaunt Through Historic Lands

Milton Henry Stine

A Winter Jaunt Through Historic Lands

ISBN/EAN: 9783337211929

Printed in Europe, USA, Canada, Australia, Japan

Cover: Foto ©Andreas Hilbeck / pixelio.de

More available books at **www.hansebooks.com**

A
WINTER JAUNT

THROUGH

HISTORIC LANDS.

EMBRACING

SCOTLAND, ENGLAND, BELGIUM, FRANCE, SWITZ-
ERLAND, ITALY, GREECE, EGYPT, AND
THE HOLY LAND,

TOGETHER WITH

PERSONAL INCIDENTS AND OBSERVATIONS.

BY

REV. MILTON H. STINE, A. M.,
AUTHOR OF LETTERS ON HOLY LAND AND "STUDIES ON THE RELIGIOUS
PROBLEM OF OUR COUNTRY."

PHILADELPHIA, PA.:
LUTHERAN PUBLICATION SOCIETY.
1890.

TO MY WIFE,

WHO TEN YEARS AGO JOINED ME ON THE WAY TO THE
"BETTER LAND,"

AND WHO HAS BEEN MY LOVING AND FAITHFUL
"COMPANION" EVER SINCE,

THIS VOLUME IS MOST AFFECTIONATELY

DEDICATED.

ILLUSTRATIONS.

	PAGE
MONUMENT OF JOHN KNOX	41
WESTMINSTER ABBEY	48
TOWER OF LONDON	52
SCENERY ON LAKE LUZERNE	63
MILAN CATHEDRAL	91
FLORENCE	97
ST. PETER'S CATHEDRAL	121
CAIRO	141
SPHINX AND PYRAMIDS	159
JERUSALEM, FROM OLIVET	208
THE DEAD SEA	261
THE JORDAN	264
BETHLEHEM	276
ABRAHAM'S OAK	281
DAMASCUS	285
ATHENS	293

INTRODUCTION.

"ANOTHER book on travel! Is it possible to say anything that has not been said many times in the countless books on this subject?" My answer is, Read and see for yourself. Scientists say, no two persons see the same object precisely the same way. So too, no two persons say the same of what they have seen and heard. For this reason there is always something new in books on travel.

The chapters in this little volume all describe old places; but what they contain will be new so long as people study history or love to travel. Whilst they may not teach much that is new, they may beguile tedious hours and create a desire to learn more of the persons, place and times of which they speak.

I did not travel as an explorer, a specialist, or a scientist. I traveled to see, to learn as much as possible of the places renowned and sites made sacred by hallowed associations. The book, however, contains the account of the most recent discoveries in the historic lands of which it speaks. As it is ever true that "Books are made from books," I wish to add that I have read "Buried Cities Recovered," "Journeyings in the Old World," "A New Path Across an Old Field," etc. These, together with my notes during my jaunt, have aided me in preparing this volume. It will be seen that a number of pages were contributed by my friends and fellow-travelers, Rev. Prof. C. B. McAfee, of Park College, Mo., and Dr. Harvey M. Kirk, of Columbus, O. These honored friends will hereby accept my thanks for their valued contributions. Hoping that this volume may be as kindly received as the one from my pen two years ago, I herewith send it on its mission, trusting that many may open it with expectation and close it with profit.

THE AUTHOR.

Lebanon, Pa., December, 1890.

CONTENTS.

PART FIRST.

EUROPE.

CHAPTER I. PAGE
Desire to travel—Preparation—Good-by—Steamer—Cargo—Company—Miss Dunn—A Storm—Entertainment on Board—Sight of Land—Bill of Fare 11-20

CHAPTER II.
Coming up the Scheldt—Irrigation—Quays—Antwerp—Walk in City—Hotel—Milk Carts—St. Jacques and Rubens—Wood-carving—Cathedral—St. Andrew's—St. Paul's—Charles V.—Brussels—Old and New—St. Gulde—Hotel de Ville—Alva and Egmont—Museum—Belgium, size of 21-30

CHAPTER III.
Glasgow—Third City in U. Kingdom—The Clyde—Description of City—University—Cathedral—Water supply—Edinburgh—In Scotch history—University—Persecution—"Bluidy Mackenzie"—Castle—Chapel of Margaret—Mons Meg—Palace—Crown-room—Cathedral—John Knox—Streets in New Town—Scott Monument—Sight by Night 31-43

CHAPTER IV.
London, on Road to—Sabbatic quiet—Spurgeon's—St. Paul's—Westminster Abbey—Parliament Buildings—The Tower—British Museum—Bank of England—Drive—St. James' Palace, etc.—Albert Memorial—Bridges—Concluding remarks 44-61

CHAPTER V.
From Brussels to Luzerne—The country and houses—Luzerne—Lake—Bridges—Cathedral—The Lion—Rigi and Pilatus—Luzerne to Milan—Grand sceneries—St. Gothard—Into Italy—Change of Scenery 61-68

(vii)

viii CONTENTS.

CHAPTER VI.

Paris—Situation and size—Boulevards—Catacombs—Bois de Boulogne Madeleine—Louvre—Palais Royal—Hotel des Invalides—Tomb of Napoleon—Cathedral—La St. Chapelle—Pantheon—St. Jacques—Bourse—Place de la Concorde—Versailles—Location—Royal palace—Rooms of Marie Antoinette—Mirror—Museum—Paintings—Gardens—Lyons—Manufactories—Cathedral—Marseilles—Quays—Streets—Cathedral—Rain and the President 69–90

CHAPTER VII.

Milan—Age—Cathedral—Spire—Nail of "True Cross"—Tomb of Borromeo—St. Ambrose—The "Brazen Serpent"—"The Last Supper by Da Vinci"—Other buildings—Florence—Scenery—Pitti Palace and Vecchio—Duomo—Campanile—Santa Croce—Amerigo Vespucci 91–101

CHAPTER VIII.

Rome—Scenery on way to—The Corso—Peasants going to town—Population and Ruins—The Forum—Arch of Titus—Mamertine Prison—Paul in Rome—Capitoline Hill—Tarpeia—Nero's palace and gardens—Baths—Fountains—Colosseum—Anecdote—Pantheon—Catacombs—Churches—St. Angelo 102–121

CHAPTER IX.

Naples—Location—Relics of Antiquity—Churches—The People—Macaroni—Funeral—Pompeii—How to get there—History—Pavement—Ruins and Population—Bodies found—Advancement in arts—Café of Diomede—On board the "Ortigia"—Sicily—Buildings, etc.—Sailing on the Mediterranean—In Africa 122–131

PART SECOND.

AFRICA AND ASIA.

CHAPTER X.

Alexandria—"Pharos"—Pilot-boats—Crowd—"Hotel Abbat"—History of City—"Pompey's Pillar"—Libraries—Christianity—Drive—Home of Antoniades—Square—Population—Merchants—Mohammedan Women—Donkeys—Scenes on the way to Cairo 132–140

CHAPTER XI.

Cairo—A donkey ride—Mosques—Slippers—Alabaster Mosque—Citadel—View—Mamelukes—"Well of Joseph"—University—"Dancing Dervishes"—Bazaars—Hotels—The street scenes—Backsheesh—Blindness and flies—Missions—The Copts 141–152

CONTENTS.			ix

PAGE
CHAPTER XII.

Boulak Museum—Arab Market—Old Statue—Raphsapha—Jewelry
—Mummies of the Pharaohs—Value of these discoveries—Road to
the Pyramids—Arabs and recommendations—Sphinx—Size—Ascent of Cheops—Scenery—Dimensions—Chamber in the Pyramid
—Who built Cheops—Memphis — Nilometer—Antiquity of Memphis—Arab village and Arab farming—Statutes of Rameses II.—
Necropolis of Egypt—Mummies of First-born—Oldest monuments
—Serapeum—Tomb of Tih—Frescoes—Way home 153-170

CHAPTER XIII.

Heliopolis — Temple — Phœnix — School of Philosophy—Obelisks—
Spring—"Virgin's Tree"—Garden of Cleopatra—Ruins at Luxor,
etc.—Addenda by Dr. Kirk—Ride up the Nile—The Nile—Asyoot
—Blindness and flies—Water lifts—Abydos—Columns—Luxor—
Thebes—Karnak—Avenue of Sphinxes—Halls—Nautch dance—
Tombs of the Pharaohs—View—Traveling on Nile—Ride through
the desert—Suez Canal—Port Said—Reflections 171-196

CHAPTER XIV.

Joppa—Our Arrival—Rolla Floyd—"House by the seaside"—Armenian Convent—The school of Miss Arnot—Orange Groves—Lutheran Colony—Tropical garden—On the Road to Jerusalem—Who
went this road—Flowers—Farming—Going to market—Ramleh—
Tower—Funeral—Dinner—View from the mountains—Abou Gosch
—Ain Karin—First view of Jerusalem 197-207

CHAPTER XV.

In the Holy City—First view—Temple plateau—Mosque of Omar—Sacred rock, etc.—Elaksa—"Solomon's stables"—Via Dolorosa—
Convent and Orphanage—Hospice of the Knights of St. John—
Church of Holy Sepulchre—Anointing slab—Where Mary stood—
Sepulchre—Place of the Crosses, etc.—House of Caiaphas—Where
the "cock crew"—Supper room—Tomb of David—Church of St.
Anne—Bethesda—General description of city 208-225

CHAPTER XVI.

A walk about Zion—View from Olivet—Mosque of the Ascension—
"Czar's Church"—Gethsemane—Virgin's Tomb—The Kedron—
Absalom's Pillar—Other tombs—Enrogel—Pools of Gihon—Quarries of Solomon—Golgotha—Church of St. Stephen—Tomb of the
Kings—Tomb of the Judges—King's Wine-presses—Land of Wonders 226-237

CONTENTS.

CHAPTER XVII.

Fulfillment of Prophecy—Spirit of improvement in the city—Industrial school—Jeremiah xxxii. 38-40—The New Jerusalem—Zech. xiv. 10—Characteristics of the new town—Conversion of the Jews. 238-246

CHAPTER XVIII.

Lepers—Where seen—Cries—Story of E. Daughan—Ancient mode of teaching lepers—Modern Leper Home—Aim of Fritz Miller—Cause Contagion 246-253

CHAPTER XIX.

Road to Jericho—Bethany—House of Simon, the leper—Tomb of Lazarus—Arab guide—Road, dangers of—View—Arab road-makers—"Apostles' Fountain"—Lunch—Dangers—View—Monastery—Brook Cherith—Modern Jericho—Jericho of Herod—Kahn—Ride to Dead Sea—On its shores—Driftwood—Life—Cities of the Plain —The ride to the Jordan—The River—Pilgrims—Bathing—The return ride—Gilgal—Ancient Jericho—Ruins—Mount of Temptation —Monasteries—Reflections 254-270

CHAPTER XX.

Hebron—Road and associations—Field of Boaz—Episode—Bethlehem —Church of the Nativity—St. Jerome—Plain of the Shepherds— "Well of David"—Memories—The people and industries—Tomb of Rachel—Giloh—"Pools of Solomon"—Aqueduct—Gardens—Cave of Adullam—Amos—Resting place—"Oak of Abraham"—View— Hebron—Age—Cave of Machpelah—Return to Jerusalem 271-284

CHAPTER XXI.

Damascus—Description—History—Paul in Damascus—Bazaars—Rugs —Silks—Blades—Great Mosque—John of Damascus, tomb of— Saladin, tomb of—Private houses—Christian Missions 284-292

CHAPTER XXII.

Athens—Drive to the city—A soldier—Language—Goods and prices— Museums—The Acropolis—The Odeon—Temple of Theseus—Of Jupiter—The Citadel-gates—The Parthenon—"Unwinged Victory"—Mars Hill 293-304

A WINTER JAUNT IN HISTORIC LANDS.

CHAPTER I.

Desire to Travel—Preparation—Good-by—Steamer—Cargo—Company—Miss Dunn—A Storm—Entertainments on Board—Sight of Land—Bill of Fare.

I NEVER knew the time that I did not have a desire to travel. In my school and college days I made many pledges to go with certain of my school-mates to the Old World. The time for carrying out the plans of my childhood and early manhood came at last.

At the request of a friend, Dr. C. F. Thomas of Philadelphia sent me an itinerary of a tour through Europe, Egypt and the Holy Land. After consulting with my wife and church council on the feasibility of my leaving home and work for three months, and carrying the matter to the Lord in prayer, I decided to go.

This was three months before the time set for my departure. It gave me ample time to read and re-read the itinerary, and to acquaint myself with many of the places I was about to visit. In making a journey of twelve thousand miles, many things must be attended to. The time was not too long, and soon the day set for my departure was painfully nigh. Had I known that it would cause those who have brought so much sunshine to my home so many anxious hours, I might have abandoned my purpose. The arrangements were now made, and it was inconvenient for many reasons to withdraw. I said most of my good-byes from a distance, and made as little of my departure as possible.

We left Jersey City at 11 a. m. February 12th. It was a delightful morning, and we had soon passed the Statue of Liberty, the Forks, and Sandy Hook, and were out at sea. We sailed on the *Noordland*, of the Red Star line. This was her fifty-second voyage. Though the *Noordland* is not one of the very largest trans-Atlantic steamers, she is a very fine boat. She is a good strong ship, 415 feet in length. The depth of her hold is 37½ feet, and her breadth is 47 feet. Her crew numbers 110 men. It costs $750 per day to pay her crew and provide all things necessary to run her. Unlike many of the large boats, she does not depend wholly on steam to run her. She has four masts, each 128 feet high. On this trip her cargo consisted of 60,000 bushels of wheat. She is capable of carrying 100,000 bushels. The *Noordland*, though so large and comfortable, is by no means the queen of ocean steamers. Shortly after the accident to the *City of Paris*, an article in the New York *Sun* gave some interesting facts concerning this great ship, a few of which we subjoin, believing them of interest to those who may read this book.*

---

* In the busy season the *City of Paris* carries about 550 first cabin, 250 second cabin, and 650 steerage passengers. There are 400 in the ship's company, including doctors, printers, boiler-makers, 6 bakers, 3 butchers, 17 cooks, hydraulic, electrical and other engineers to the number of 32, 148 stewards and 8 stewardesses. So there may be about 1,850 aboard.

Notwithstanding the fact that many of the passengers are sea-sick from the time they pass Sandy Hook until Fastnet is sighted, they manage to consume in one trip something like 13,000 pounds of fresh beef, 3,000 pounds of corned beef, 4,000 pounds of mutton, 1,000 pounds of lamb, 2,000 pounds of veal and pork, 15,000 pounds of bacon, 500 pounds of liver, tripe and sausages, 200 hams, 300 pounds of fish, 20,000 eggs, 17 tons of potatoes, 3 tons of other vegetables, 3,600 pounds of butter, 600 pounds of cheese, 600 pounds of coffee, 350 pounds of tea, 100 pounds of icing sugar, 150 pounds of powdered sugar, 670 pounds of loaf sugar, 3,000 pounds of moist sugar, 700 pounds

Our company consisted of fifteen ministers of the Gospel, belonging to six different denominations, twelve laymen, among whom were lawyers, doctors and merchants, and fourteen ladies. One of the ladies, Miss Dunn of Pittsburg, was on her way to Jerusalem as a missionary. The career of Miss Dunn is somewhat remarkable, hence a word with regard to her may be of interest.

My attention was called to this lady at Jersey

---

of salt, 200 pounds of nuts, 560 pounds of dried fruit, 20 barrels of apples, 3,600 lemons, 20 cases of oranges—and other green fruit in season--300 bottles of pickles, 150 bottles of ketchup, sauce, and horse radish, and 150 cans of preserves.

There are also quantities of poultry, oysters, sardines, canned vegetables, and soups, vinegar, pepper, mustard, curry, rice, tapioca, sago, hominy, oatmeal, molasses, condensed milk, "tinned" Boston beans, confectionery and ice cream. Fifty pounds of ice cream are served at a single meal in the first cabin.

Thirty tons of ice are required to keep the great storerooms cool. Eight barrels of flour are used daily. The bakers are busy from dawn of day. They make 4,000 delicious Parker House rolls for breakfast every morning. Thirty eight-pound loaves of white bread and one hundred pounds of brown bread are baked each day; also, pies, puddings, cakes, etc.

Eight barrels of common crackers and a hundred tins of fancy crackers are stowed away in the storeroom, together with 100 pounds of wine and plum cake, not a crumb of which is

City, about an hour before the boat left her pier. On hearing the voice of song on the starboard, my wife and a friend, together with others, went over to hear the music, and to see the persons who sang. We found a company of men and women engaged in a solemn and impressive farewell to their sister in Christ. On the second day out, I obtained an introduction to her, when she gave me the following account of her life:

---

left when Liverpool is reached. Six thousand bottles of ale and porter, 4,200 bottles of mineral waters, 4,500 bottles of wine, and more or less ardent spirits, are drunk inside of six days by the guests of this huge floating hotel. About 3,000 cigars are sold [on board, but many more are smoked. Two hundred pounds of toilet soap are supplied by the steamship company.

One of the odd sights to be seen on the double-decked Inman pier soon after the arrival of the "queen of the ocean greyhounds" is the great stacks of soiled linen which are being assorted by about a dozen stewards. Here is the wash-list for a single trip: Napkins, 8,300; tablecloths, 180; sheets, 3,600; pillow-cases, 4,400; towels, 16,200, and dozens of blankets and counterpanes. Although the list is very short, it requires four large two-horse trucks to carry the wash to the Inman Company's steam laundry in Jersey City. In less than a week it is back in the lockers of the linen rooms, which are in charge of a regular linen-keeper. There is no washing done aboard. Many of the ship's company have their washing done in New York, but the greater number have it done in Liverpool.

She was born in Pittsburg, Pa., was educated and became a teacher. On her conversion she resolved to become a missionary; but on being examined by the physician, it was found that her lungs were badly diseased. She became worse, and her life was despaired of. She herself now confided her health to the Lord. She was fully resolved to live or die, as the Master should see fit. She had no sooner done this than she resolved to rise from her bed. In a month from this time she went to her parents' home, where she steadily gained in health.

Christ seemed more precious to her now than ever before, and she once more consecrated herself to the service of Foreign Missions. But she was without means and without friends. The Lord, however, opened the way for her, and she went to a training school in New York City. She worked hard, and at the end of the first year stood first in the class, winning all the prizes. A position was offered her during her summer vacation in the Berachah Orphanage in New York City, an institution which supports 200 orphans. This home has no endowment, but like the homes founded by George Müller, depends upon voluntary contributions, which always come in answer to prayer.

When her vacation was over, she was offered a permanent position in the Home. She was anxious to return to school, but her funds were exhausted, so she asked time for consideration. A few days afterwards she received a letter from an acquaintance who did not believe in foreign missions; but he said he felt it a duty to support her one year in school. The offer was accepted, and at the end of the year Miss Dunn graduated. She now became the matron in the Berachah Orphanage, where she remained one year. During the year she resolved to go to Jerusalem to work among the Jews. This resolution she is now in the act of carrying into effect. She goes independent of any Society, relying wholly upon the Lord for support. She did not know until within a few weeks, where she might find a home in Palestine. Some one who is interested in the work at Bethany, on hearing of Miss Dunn's purpose, offered her a home in this historical village until the Lord directs her farther.

The first three days of our voyage were beautiful and warm as May. The ocean was "calm as a cradled child in dreamless slumber bound." Friday was the loveliest St. Valentine any of us ever saw, but as the morning mail did not arrive, we received no valentines. Saturday the wind was from the south, and sailing was not so pleasant as it had been. Sunday it was still worse. The weather became more unpleasant until February 18, when the wind blew a gale from the northwest. The heaviest storm the *Noordland* had experienced in this winter of storms was now upon us. "How the giant element leaped with delirious bound!"

The sea and sky seemed to sweep in one awful mass toward the boat. The rain and hail fell in torrents. The waves seemed to mount high above the vessel, and then of a sudden they would raise her in their mighty arms and toss her as you would a child. Again they would dash upon the main deck, having swept the port-holes with a roar and a frightful whirl. They deluged the main deck, and dashed the spray into the face of the watch on the bridges. The mighty ship groaned as she now tunneled or mounted the billows. The storm roared and the top yard broke from its fastenings. This caused the sail to fly to and fro with the noise of thunder. A dozen sailors in the rain and storm climbed with the agility of cats up the rope-ladders, and with herculean effort succeeded in furling the sail. In the ship men and women staggered to and fro. They could not sit unless they held on with might and main. When they lay down they rolled to and fro like balls. At the table at dinner all was in commotion. The few who were well enough to eat emptied soup-dishes into their laps. Water-bottles slipped hither and thither, knives and forks jingled, and nothing remained where you put it. But the storm was soon over. For the last four days of our eleven days' voyage the sea was again comparatively calm. On the morning of the tenth day we sighted Point Lizard. All of us were glad to see the land, but it was thirty-six hours before we put our feet on shore at Antwerp.

Notwithstanding the storm and sea-sickness we did not have the dreary time on board one might suppose. We had an almost constant flow of wit and wisdom. Every evening we had an entertainment. Some of the passengers who had been abroad before read accounts of their trips, others gave us select readings, instrumental and vocal music. Of course, we had a daily prayer-meeting whenever practicable.

A sea-voyage, therefore, is not monotonous—although beyond seeing a sail now and then, and viewing the sun rise and set, there is nothing to attract attention. I saw the sun rise one morning before the storm. First, there was a crescent of fire in the sea; this grew rapidly until it became a sphere, when it elongated into a balloon of fire with the basket hidden in the sea; then it became the full orb of day, as we have it on land.

We have always had plenty so eat, but not a few were unable to come to the saloon for a great part of the voyage. I missed only one meal in the saloon. I subjoin the bill of fare for one dinner: "Mock turtle soup, bon din of bologna with craffles, boiled salmon trout, Dutch sauce, braized brisket of beef flamande, fricassee of chicken, veal cutlets with tomato sauce, roast leg of mutton, red currant jelly, spinach, larded sweetbreads, roast pigeon compote, plum pudding, brandy sauce, strawberry ice cream, fruits assorted, coffee."

CHAPTER II.

Coming up Scheldt—Irrigation—Quays—Antwerp—Walk in—Hotel—Milk Carts—St. Jacques and Rubens—Wood Carving—Cathedral—St. Andrews—St. Paul's—Charles V.—Brussels Old and New—St. Gulde—Hotel de Ville—Alva and Egmont Museum—Belgium, Size, etc.

IN coming up the Scheldt one is impressed with the fact that he is sailing on a body of water that is really higher than the surrounding landscape. Immense dykes keep the sea from encroaching on the land. The country is irrigated by ditches which extend from the streams through well cultivated fields. Such a thorough irrigation prevents the crops from suffering in a drought. As the vessel went up the stream, girls in short skirts, big wooden shoes, and with their heads tied up in shawls, came out of low stone houses to look at us and welcome us by the waving of handkerchiefs.

The magnificent quays along the shore are, to a large extent, the work of Napoleon I. Many of the fine docks were demolished in 1814; but two great basins were preserved. These have been converted into docks, and are now lined with warehouses. Antwerp itself is a very old city, having been founded in the seventh century. In the fifteenth and sixteenth centuries it had attained the zenith of its prosperity. From this time to the close of the long wars with Spain and France and the Netherlands, the city declined in population and commerce. At present it is the principal seaport of Belgium, if not of the continent. It has a population of 176,000. It was quite dark on the Sabbath of February 23d when we landed. After passing the Custom House officers, which was readily done, we drove to the beautiful hotel St. Antoine. This hotel is built after the manner of most hotels in Europe and the East, in the shape of a square with an open centre. A marble pavement surrounds the court. This pavement is protected from the weather by a glass casement. The dining rooms are large and very pretty. There are open fire-places in the sleeping rooms, but the fires are extra. It was already late in the evening, after we had dinner, but a number of us took a walk. We walked both to see the town and to try the novelty of walking on shore after having been on the sea more than eleven days. It was Sunday evening, and the close of the Carnival. This may account for the fact that we passed several drunken men, a brass band and a company of masqueraders. We were so very tired that our walk was short.

Early on Monday morning we were ready for sight-seeing. The first objects of interest were the milk carts and small wagons drawn by dogs followed by a peasant, a woman usually, with her great wooden shoes, short skirts and bare head. These women assist their dogs by pushing the cart from behind. The men generally take the more easy part by following the carts at some distance, leisurely smoking their pipes. One sees few wagons in Belgium. The hauling is done mostly with carts, to which a horse or dog is attached. The horses here, as in France and England, are large, fine brutes.

There are a number of places of interest in Antwerp. We first visited the grave of Rubens, in the church of St. Jacques. Rubens, though a German by birth, spent much of his time in Antwerp. Here are his earliest, and according to most critics, his masterpieces. The "Descent from the Cross" is the finest painting that ever came from his brush. This is in the cathedral in this city. Rubens was a hard worker. He painted, with the assistance of his students 1,800 pictures, an average of one per week throughout his entire career. He died in Antwerp, in May, 1640, in the sixty-third year of his age, the greatest master of the Flemish school. The church of St. Jacques is old, and is famous only as the burial place of Rubens. It contains a window made of beautiful stained glass of the first half of the seventeenth century. It likewise has several grand altars. The Jesuits' chapel, not far from St. Jacques, is famous for its wood-carvings by Von Brunt. There is nothing in the world in this art which excels the rich wood-carvings in Antwerp and Brussels. St. Jacques belonged to the monastery which still stands close by. The building is Gothic, the arches resting on immense stone pillars.

Of all churches in Antwerp the cathedral is the most famous, first, because it is the finest Gothic edifice in Europe, and secondly, because it contains the masterpieces of Rubens. This church was finished a century before the discovery of America, but the tooth of time has had little effect on its great massive walls. The stone floors are worn by the footsteps of the thousands who have been in the habit of coming to the grand old church during all these years. The spire is 403 feet high. The work on the tower is so delicate that it looks like lace from the street below. Napoleon, it is said, was so impressed with its beauty that he said the whole ought to be covered with a glass case. The view from the top of this tower is superb. Its chimes are among the finest in the world. The principal paintings in the church are the "Descent from the Cross," the "Elevation of the Cross," "The Assumption," and "The Resurrection." In the "Elevation" Rubens has painted a picture of himself in armor. He frequently painted pictures of his wife to represent the Virgin. The picture of "The Assumption" was painted in sixteen days. He received $640 for the work. "The Descent" was stolen by Napoleon I., but, like most of the Emperor's stolen property, was afterwards returned. There is also a picture entitled "Christ in the Temple" in the Cathedral, but it is not famous. Of all paintings in Antwerp the "Descent from the Cross" impressed me most. There is the gaping spear-wound in the side, the blood still oozing out. So natural does it seem that one feels a strong impulse to spring forward and hold his handkerchief over the wound whilst the lifeless body is being lowered. The whole is so realistic that to see the picture is to remember it forever. The seats in the Cathedral, as in all the cathedrals of Europe, are movable. They consist mainly of splint chairs, with a little shelf attached to the rear for the person on the seat behind to support his hymn-book. These chairs are readily moved from one altar to another, inasmuch as mass is celebrated before the various altars at different times.

The church of St. Andrews has the finest pulpit in the world. It is a rich piece of oak carving. The Master walks upon the sea. Andrew and Peter are in the boat. Behind them is a background, also carved, to represent a rocky coast, with the trunk of a tree in the foreground. Above these there is a canopy, on the one side of which are cherubs holding a tapestry in graceful folds. Two other cherubs are holding upright a St. Andrew's cross. It must be remembered that all this is carved out of solid oak. The art gallery not far from the Cathedral has many fine paintings, principally by Rubens, Vandyke and Keiser. This museum of art belongs to the city. The managers recently published two portraits exhibited in Paris last summer, for which they paid the neat sum of $35,000.

The Church of St. Paul is also worthy of a visit. The confessionals in this church are beautiful carvings in oak. On the outside of the church there is a representation of Calvary. The walk which leads to the mount on the side of the church is skirted by stone walls. On these walls are statues of the Apostles. Adjacent to the church is the representation of Christ in the tomb, which is very realistic. Above this Mary holds the dead Christ on her knees. Others are standing near, their faces wearing expressions of the deepest sympathy. Still higher stands the cross with Christ upon it. The large stones placed at intervals in the walks were brought from Jerusalem.

The mansion of Charles V. faces an open square in the most beautiful part of the city. It is a building six stories high, standing like a ghost to personate that king's cunning, cruelty and treachery. The building is now used as a warehouse.

Among other places of interest in the historical old city are the public library, the botanical and zoölogical gardens, the bourse, the bank, the home of Rubens, the monuments and the public parks. One can well spend weeks in Antwerp without tiring.

From Antwerp we went to Brussels. The two cities are only twenty-nine miles apart. The ride is through a beautiful country, well cultivated. In fifty-nine minutes we had made the distance and were safely landed in Brussels. There is a new and an old town. The former contains the royal palaces, the finest park in the city, the public promenade, the palace of justice, the libraries, and the museums. The principal church is the St. Gulde. It is a large edifice with two high towers. The choir and transept were finished in 1273. The whole exterior was restored in 1843. This church is famous for its rich stained glass-windows. The pulpit is a fine specimen of oak carving, and by some believed superior to that in St. Andrews in Antwerp. There are statues of the twelve Apostles, and many costly monuments erected in memory of the Duke of Brabant.

The Hotel de Ville dates its beginning to that of the fifteenth century, and is one of the finest buildings in Brussels. The tower is very fine, and rises to the height of 364 feet. The vane on the tower is a figure of St. Michael in gilded copper, and is seventeen feet high. In the same square upon which the Hotel de Ville is situated is the building in which Count Egmont spent his last night on earth. Where he met his death his statue and that of the Count of Horn now stand. These ever remind the reader of the account of the perfidy of the Duke of Alva, who after having promised Egmont protection, and having received his presents, basely condemned him to death, and watched the tragedy from a window overlooking the whole scene.

Brussels has a public library containing 25,000 volumes and 20,000 MSS. The collection of paintings in the museum, once the residence of the Spanish and Austrian governors, are famous. The paintings are all the work of one man, who is said to have been partly demented. There is a scene from Homer's Iliad. Another represents the soul leaving the body, in three scenes—first, a human form, then the soul leaving the form, then the form a corpse and the soul a shadow at its side. Another painting represents Napoleon in hell. He is met by the widows whose husbands he destroyed. Next come the husbands and brothers whom he slew in battle; their fists are clenched and their faces wear bitter scowls. The scene is horrible. There is another, of a man raising the lid from the coffin in which he was placed before he was actually dead. To see the cadaverous face with its expression of horror is to remember it forever.

Brussels in the newer part is noted for its clean wide streets and its fine buildings. As a manufacturing city it excels in the making of fine lace, leather, linen and woolen goods, earthenware, chemicals, carriages, and steam engines. In short, it takes rank among the first cities in Europe in its manufactories. The whole kingdom of Belgium is a little more than one-fourth as large as the State of Pennsylvania, but it sustains a population nearly twice as large. It has played an important part in the history of Europe. French is the language of the educated. Most of the peasantry speak Flemish. The country is not distinguished for its natural scenery. It is level and well cultivated.

We left Belgium at 7 a. m. on February 25th, for Switzerland and Italy, well pleased with what we had seen of the first country we visited in Europe.

CHAPTER III.

GLASGOW—Third City in United Kingdom—The Clyde—Description of City—University—Cathedral—Water Supply.
EDINBURGH—In Scotch History—The University—Persecutions—"Bluidy Mackenzie"—The Castle—Chapel of Margaret—Mons Meg—The Palace—The Crown-room—The Cathedral—John Knox—Streets in New Town—Scott Monument—Sight by Night.

I HAD a good jaunt through the great commercial city of Scotland just before I embarked for America, having come from Alexandria in Egypt by way of Messina and Corsica to Marseilles, and from thence to Paris, London and Edinburgh. For evident reasons I prefer to speak of these cities before I take the reader to France, Italy, Egypt and Syria.

Glasgow is the third city in the United Kingdom, and has a population of nearly one million souls. The ship-building interests on the Clyde are the most extensive in the world. The river Clyde is a narrow stream, and is always filled with great ships, which come from every country in the world. We came near having a collision on our way down the stream. How collisions can be avoided in this crowded stream is a mystery to me.

The residences of Glasgow are very fine. The old part of the town lies along the river, but the newer and finer part of the city stretches up to the rolling ground. Here are fine parks surrounding wealthy gentlemen's houses. Near the centre of the city is George's Square. Here is an equestrian statue of Queen Victoria, statues of Walter Scott, the poet Campbell, Sir John Moore, Lord Clyde and others also adorn the square. The university, established in 1868, is an immense structure, covering six acres of ground. It has ninety-eight departments of instruction, and is destined to become one of the finest institutions of learning in Europe. The Cathedral is the most interesting structure in this city. Its foundations were laid nearly 800 years ago, upon the site occupied by a church built by St. Mungo five hundred years earlier. Originally it was a Roman Catholic place of worship; then it became the property of the Episcopalians. When the Presbyterian church became the established church, her ministers preached in this edifice. There are many famous tombs within its sacred walls. The city receives its water supply from Lake Katrine, immortalized by Sir Walter Scott.

This water is of an excellent quality. There are many fine stores on the long, broad street. The people are polite, hardy and industrious.

From Glasgow to Edinburgh is a pleasant two hours' ride by express train through a delightful country. Edinburgh is an old, and to the Scotch a sacred city. It has been called the Athens and the Jerusalem of Scotland. It has been noted for its culture and its bravery for many centuries. There are few cities in Europe where there is more to admire and to interest than in the capital of Scotland. "Nothing can state its infinite variety, and whatever the tastes of the individual are—whether antiquarian, romantic, picturesque or scholarly—they can all be satiated within a stone's throw of the castle-crowned crag that towers monarch-like over the city." One can spend days of profit and of pleasure in its palaces, its churches, and its historical places.

Some of the oldest institutions in this historic city are by no means mere relics for the antiquarian. They have the progressive spirit of the nineteenth century. Among these is the University, which now has more than one thousand students. It was chartered by James VI. of Scotland in 1582. It is one of the finest institutions of learning in the world. Its library is one of the most select and perfect in Europe. Besides the university, Edinburgh has a High-school which cost $250,000. In this city was fought many a battle for the faith. It was the scene of martyrdom for the cause of Christ. From 1661, in which year Argyle was beheaded, to February, 1688, there were destroyed 18,000 people. Of these, about 100 were killed in Edinburgh. These people were true to their country's highest good. They were true to their faith, preferring death rather than worshipping God contrary to the dictates of their consciences. In the antiquarian museum the guillotine with which the Covenanters were beheaded is still to be seen. There are the thumb-screws by means of which they extorted confession from their hapless victims. By browbeating and torture, James Duke of York, Dalziel and Graham of Claverhouse tried the passive heroism of the confessors. Sir George Mackenzie, as the king's advocate, was so zealous in persecuting those who were apprehended that he received the ignoble title of "bluidy Mackenzie." For many years after his death the boys went to his tomb and called into the keyhole

"Bluidy Mackenzie, come out if ye daur,
Lift the sneck and draw the bar."

The population of Edinburgh is at present about 250,000. For centuries it was a little town consisting of a few straw-thatched huts occupying a part of the middle ridge of the three hills upon which the modern city is built. Then in the days of Mary of Guise it consisted of a "dense array of tall stone fabrics extending along the top of the hill to the palace of Holyrood, more than a mile in length." The tall piles, the lofty spires and the grand old rock gave it an impressive appearance.

Among the prominent objects of interest to-day is the old castle. This huge stone pile is perched on the summit of a rock 443 feet high. Upon this rock men lived long before the authentic records of Scotland began. Previous to the siege of 1573 the eastern front of the fortress must have been picturesque in the extreme. Mr. W. Chambers, in describing the castle as it then was, says: "The principal and central object was a donjon or keep, rising 60 feet above the summit of the rock, and known by the name of David's Tower, having been erected by David II. between 1367 and 1371. From the palace, a curtain wall extended northward along the front of the rock to this tower, from which it again passed on in the same direction to a somewhat smaller tower, the remains of which still exist embedded in the present half-moon battery; Onward from this smaller one the wall went northwards till it reached another tower of greater importance, called the Constable's Tower, being the residence of that officer, and which rose 50 feet high from the rocky platform, exactly over the site of the present portcullis gate, and accessible by a stair ascending the face of the rock, which formed the sole means of reaching the citadel or upper platform of the castle. In the siege above referred to, five batteries played for nine days upon the eastern front, and wrought such ruin that David's Tower and the Constable's being wholly beaten down, all passage out or in was debarred by the mass of *débris;* and the gallant Kirkcaldy and his brave companions, when they surrendeded, had to be let down over the front by a rope. The whole of the present eastern front was constructed by the Regent Morton immediately after the siege."

On this hill is the chapel of Queen Margaret. It was built in the eleventh century. It is the smallest and the oldest chapel in Scotland, measuring only $16\frac{1}{2}$ feet by $10\frac{1}{2}$ feet. It is interesting with its single window and its rough walls of mighty stone, because it teaches us what privations even kings and queens endured in those days in their public and private life. The old gun Mons Meg is quite a curiosity. Some say it was "forged at Mons, in Belgium, in 1476, while others assert that it was fabricated in Galloway, and used by James II. at the siege of Thrieve Castle in 1455. But however that may be, it is known to have been employed by James IV. at the siege of Dumbarton in 1489, and at that of Norham Castle, on the Borders, in 1497. It burst when firing a salute in honor of the Duke of York in 1682; was removed to the tower of London in 1754; but was restored to Scotland (mainly at the intercession of Sir Walter Scott) by command of King George IV. in 1829. This large cannon is formed of long pieces of malleable iron, held together by strong hoops of the same material. It is 13 feet long, 20 inches in diameter."*

On this same hill is the ancient palace which for centuries formed the home and stronghold of the kings and queens of Scotland. The room in which James II. of England was born is pointed out on the ground floor. The original ceiling of the room is still to be seen. On the wall is the royal arms. Beneath is the following:

---
*"Guide to Edinburgh."

"Lord Jesu Christ, that crounit was with Thornse,
Preserve the Birth, quhais Badgie heir is borne,
And send Hir Sonne successione, to Reign stille,
Long in this Realm, if that it be thy will.
Als grant, O Lord, quhat ever of Hir proceed,
Be to Thy Honer, and Praise, sobied.
19th IVNII, 1566."

The crown room contains the crown with which the kings of the realm were crowned. The sceptre is of solid silver. It is 34 inches long, and is surmounted by statues of the Virgin, St. Andrew and St. James. Here too is a sword which Pope Julius II. presented to James IV. A ruby ring set with diamonds and worn by Charles I. at his coronation is also shown in this room. All these royal relics are under a glass case.

Everybody who goes to Edinburgh visits Holyrood House, where once the kings of Scotland lived. It is now "a deserted palace, where no monarch dwells." The picture gallery is a large room, and contains imaginary portraits of kings of Scotland, real and fictitious. These portraits were painted 200 years ago. The most interesting apartments in the palace are the rooms of Queen Mary, the beautiful, the blameworthy, and the unfortunate queen of the Scots. Her furniture is still there. Even the moth-eaten and decayed curtains, once of the richest damask silk, are on the fastenings as the servants of the queen left them. In the small closet adjoining the bed chamber David Rizzio was murdered. Darnley and his co-conspirators gained access by a secret stairway. As we look upon these rooms we can only exclaim,

> "The boast of heraldry, the pomp of power,
>   And all that beauty, all that wealth ever gave,
>   Await alike the inevitable hour ;
>   The paths of glory lead but to the grave."

The chapel royal or Abbey of Holyrood was founded in 1128. It is now a ruin. Here Mary was married to Darnley. Kings and queens were crowned here, but its glory has departed. It is eloquent in its ruins.

Another place of interest is the Cathedral. A church is said to have stood here as early as the ninth century. In 1466, at which time there were forty altars within its walls, together with an armbone of St. Giles (after whom the church is named), James III. made it a collegiate church. At the Reformation the building was divided into four separate places of worship. The section east of the transept, now known as High Church, was made the parish church of the city, and John

Knox was appointed pastor. It was here, in July 1565, that he delivered the bold speech against Mary's marriage with Darnley, whom Randolph, an English ambassador, calls "an intolerable fool," and who was a libertine and unworthy of the beautiful and unfortunate Mary queen of Scots. At that time this bold preacher denounced the nobles and others for their inactivity in the matter. "I see," said he, suddenly stretching out his arms, as if he would leap from the pulpit and arrest the passing vision, "I see before me your beleaguered camp. I hear the tramp of the horsemen as they charge you in the streets,"—and in a strain of lofty and sustained eloquence he denounced, exhorted, and warned his hearers, with such vehemence, says Melvil, that "he was like to ding [dash] the pulpit in blads [splinters] and flee out of it!" *

Knox was for ten years a priest. He was in England four years, but Scotland gave him his fame. He was a mighty champion of the truth. The old pulpit from which he spoke with such power is still to be seen in the antiquarian museum. Between the Cathedral and Parliament buildings there is a brown stone about a foot and

---

* "Guide to Edinburgh."

MONUMENT OF JOHN KNOX, EDINBURGH.

a half square, with the following in brass raised letters,

I. K.

1572.

Here it is said repose the mortal remains of the great reformer of Scotland.

At the head of the street called Canongate still stands the house in which Knox lived. It consists of three rooms, a study, a sitting-room and a bedroom. The second story is reached by a flight of steps on the outside. Running across the whole width of the building, above the door of the lower story, is the following: "Lufe, God. Abufe, Al. And Yi Nychtbour, As, Yi Self."

From Calton Hill, off Princess Street, one has a magnificent view of Prince Arthur's Seat, of the city and the new bridge across the Frith of Forth, twelve miles away. There are monuments of Burns, Playfair, Dugald Stewart and Nelson on this hill; also an unfinished structure which is intended to commemorate the Scotch who fell in the battles consequent to the French Revolution.

Edinburgh consists of a new and old part. It is with regard to the new town that I wish now to speak. The railroad runs between the two towns, so called. For quite a distance on both sides of the railroad is a deep ravine. In this ravine and on the slopes on either side there are fine trees, beautiful walks, and flower-plots tastily arranged. In this park, on the Princess Street side, is the monument of Sir Walter Scott. It was erected in 1840-44 at a cost of $75,000. It is in the form of an open crucial Gothic spire, supported on four grand early English arches, which serve as a canopy to the statue, and is about 200 feet high. A staircase in the interior of one of the columns leads to a series of galleries, to which visitors are admitted on payment of two-pence. Under the central basement arch is a marble statue, by Steell, of Sir Walter, with a figure of his favorite dog Maida at his feet; it was inaugurated in 1846, and cost £2000. In the niches above the several arches are figures of some of the leading characters in his works. The architect was a self-taught genius named George Meikle Kemp, the son of a shepherd at Newhall, on the southern slope of the Pentland Hills, near Edinburgh, who was accidentally drowned in the Union Canal before the work was completed. Immediately to the west is a bronze statue, the work of Mr. Hutchinson, R. S. A., erected to the memory of Adam Black, Lord Provost and M. P. for the city, and publisher of the *Encyclopædia Britannica.**

Princess Street is one of the finest streets not only in Edinburgh, but in all England. In fact, all the streets of the new town are wide, well paved and clean. The buildings are massive stone structures. There is a uniformity in the buildings of different blocks which is carried out in the minutest detail. From my hotel (the Royal) I had a beautiful view of the old town. The streets there rise in terraces. At night when the whole hill is illuminated by lights on the streets and in the buildings, the effect is very pretty. On the hill there, some of the most momentous events in Scotch history occurred. Events there transpired which are as brilliant in the galaxy of the histories of nations as the hillside with its myriad lights in the night time. May the sons and daughters continue to prize what was purchased at so great a cost, is the wish of the author of this little volume.

---

*" Guide to Edinburgh."

CHAPTER IV.

London, on Road to—Sabbatic Quiet—Spurgeon's—St. Paul's—Westminster Abbey—Parliament Buildings—The Tower—British Museum—Bank of England—Drive—St. James' Palace—Albert Memorial—Bridges—Concluding Remarks.

FROM Edinburgh to London is an eight hours' ride on one of the best-equipped roads in the United Kingdom, if not in the world. The cars are wide and comfortable when compared with some in which I have ridden in Egypt and the Continent. The time made by the Flying Dutchman, the Flying Irishman, and the Flying Scotchman, as the three express trains on the London Northwestern are called, is excellent, and so well are these trains managed that one scarcely ever hears of an accident.

It was Sunday morning when we arrived in London. The sky was clear; for once there was no fog either in the city or its environments. We instinctively felt that we were really in God's country. Everywhere in the country and the small towns outside the great city people neatly attired, with hymn-books in their hands, were on their way to church. Soon after a good breakfast at the "Covent Garden" hotel we started for Spurgeon's tabernacle. In the yard we were handed an envelope, into which we put a small contribution and deposited it in a box, also in the yard. We entered the church by a side door. It is an immense structure, one hundred and thirty-six feet long. It has four aisles and three rows of seats, and two galleries which run entirely around the house. Take an egg and cut down a bit of its side, place it on this side, then put two galleries around it; put the rostrum on a level with the first gallery at the narrower end of it, and you have a good idea of the interior of Spurgeon's tabernacle. The usher puts you on a side seat until ten minutes before the beginning of the service, when all pews not filled by the regular renters are at the service of the public. The deacons are very polite, and have a word and hand-shake for everybody. Promptly on time the great preacher enters. There is nothing very marked about him—ponderous, red-faced, kind-looking. I knew him from his picture when I saw him speaking to one of his deacons in the aisle. The service was opened by a short, impressive prayer; then a hymn was announced. A man at Spurgeon's side led the song. There is no choir.

The vast audience of 4000 joined the song. The time was execrable, but the singing was impressive. After singing, the great man led in prayer. He literally talked with God. His Scripture reading and his prayer impressed me much more than his sermon. He read the account of the healing of the man born blind, and interspersed his reading with frequent and appropriate comments. He preached on the words "Dost thou believe on the Son of God?" I for one went away not a little profited.

In the afternoon our company attended service in St. Paul's Cathedral. We listened to Canon Liddon. Being seated just beyond the transept, much of the sermon was lost through the echo. The singing by an immense choir immediately in front of the speaker was very fine. The vast edifice was nearly full, thus showing that not all churches in England are empty.

St. Paul's is the fifth largest cathedral in the world. The present building was begun in 1675. The plans were made by the celebrated Christopher Wren. The building is in the form of a Latin cross, and cost nearly four million dollars. Already in the time of Constantine a Christian church occupied the site of the present cathedral. We read accounts of the restoration of a building or buildings on this ground as early as 610, 961 and 1087. St. Paul's is beautiful in the highest sense of the word. The distance from the street to the top of the dome is 404 feet. The cross and the ball on the top of the dome weigh nearly half a ton. In the cupola, 260 feet from the street, is the famous whispering gallery. A whisper on the one side of the gallery is distinctly heard on the other side, a distance of 108 feet. In the dome the visitor has an excellent view of the ceiling painted by Thornhill. It is said while the great artist was at work he stepped steadily backward in viewing his painting, when he reached the edge of the scaffold and would certainly have fallen had not an assistant dashed his brush upon the work, which broke the spell and caused the artist to spring forward, thus saving his life. St. Paul's has nearly a hundred monuments. The ashes of Lord Wellington and Lord Nelson, two of England's greatest generals, lie buried here.

In the evening of the same day we visited Westminster Abbey. Cannon Farrar was out of town, but it did not matter to us. The crowd was so large that I stood in the Poets' Corner for a little while, then went out, and after a brief walk went

A WINTER JAUNT IN HISTORIC LANDS. 49

"The cloud-capped towers,
The gorgeous palaces,
The solemn temples
The great globe, itself, yea
All which it inherits,
Shall dissolve
And like the baseless
Fabric of a vision,
Leave not a wreck behind."

John Gay's tribute is from his own writings,

"Life is a FEST, and all things show it;
I thought so once, but now I know it."

The tribute to the Wesleys consists of a marble slab having upon it the faces of the two brothers and the following: "John Wesley was born June 17th, 1703, died March 2d, 1791. Charles Wesley, born December 18th, 1708, died March 29th, 1788. The best of all, God is with us."

Below is a figure of Wesley preaching and the words, "I look upon all the world as my parish. God buries his workmen, but carries on his work."

The number of epitaphs and inscriptions is almost infinite in the grand old edifice.

The names of kings, jurists, theologians, reformers, philosophers and poets are recorded there in every form that can be imagined. The oldest tomb in the abbey is that of King Sebert, dated A. D. 616. There is a Roman sarcophagus here which was found under one of the tombs in 1869. The shield and helmet worn by the Black Prince are placed over the chapel of Henry VII. Dean Stanley's is one of the latest tombs in this great house of the dead. Our own Longfellow's name is recorded in the Poets' Corner. Of this house it may well be said, the very walls are eloquent. The stones in the floor upon which you tread nearly all contain a record of some great name. It is a place in which one might spend months with profit.

Close to Westminster Abbey are the new houses of Parliament. These buildings cover an area of eight acres, and contain 1100 apartments, 100 staircases, and two miles of corridors. The foundation stone of these structures was laid April 27th, 1840. The House of Lords is one of the finest halls in the world. It contains the throne for the queen. A woolsack (a chair cushioned with wool) in the centre of the hall is the place where the Lord Chancellor sits. The floor is a pavement of fine mosaics; the ceiling is in gilded panels. The whole is spoiled by the extreme height of the ceiling. The ends of the chamber contain beautiful frescoes. There are twelve figures in the glass-stained windows, of barons who compelled King John to grant the Magna Charta. The queen's entrance is through the tower bearing her name. The cellars of the building are always examined two hours before the queen's arrival, so that the place may be safe for her majesty. The House of Commons contains nothing of special note. The outside of the building is blackened by the soot and smoke, which deface all buildings in London. On the side facing the square are the statues of the kings of England in niches. The stone of this magnificent structure, it is said, is already yielding to the tooth of time. The roof is finely docorated; the great clock in the tower has four dials thirty feet in diameter. The building cost upward of $20,000,000.

Everybody who comes to London visits the famous London Tower. This is an old place, dating back to the days of Julius Cæsar. Its present buildings cover twelve acres. It includes the barracks, the armory containing 60,000 stand of arms, the White Tower, Jewel Tower, Bloody Tower, the Brick Tower, and the Beauchamp Tower. Ever since its erection it has figured prominently in English history. At one time it was the royal residence. Stephen is the first monarch mentioned as having resided in this place. When we arrived at the Tower we were compelled to hand our satchels and parcels to the guard, for fear that their contents might be dangerous. The English are terribly afraid of dynamite. The guards here are dressed in the uniform of the Middle Ages. It consists of a big black hat, a coat with a gathered skirt, and a rosette. We passed the gateway of the Tower of Richard II., known as the traitor's gate, because traitors were taken through this way to the place of execution. We passed over the stairs underneath which the bones of Edward V. and those of his brother were found, to St. John's chapel, where the king and suite used to worship; then into the banquet hall, where Richard III. condemned Hastings; then into the council chamber where Guy Fawkes was examined. This room is filled with armor of the sixteenth century. Here we saw the mask of Will Sommers, court jester of Henry VIII. Here too is an exact image of Queen Elizabeth on horseback and of her page, as they appeared when they went to St. Paul's to give thanks at the destruction of the Armada. Near by is the cloak on which Wolfe died at Quebec.

We next went into the torture chamber under the Tower, the walls of which are 14 feet in thick-

TOWER OF LONDON.

ness. The holes in the floor indicate the place where the rack was located. Opposite the entrance is a small room, "Little Ease," not large enough to lie down in. Here Guy Fawkes was confined seven weeks. Through this chamber we enter the crypt under St. John's chapel, where, without light or comfort, as high as three hundred prisoners were kept at one time. Quitting this, we went where the scaffold for private execution used to be located. Here Anne Boleyn and Lady Jane Grey were executed. After witnessing a drill of redcoats we went to Beauchamp Tower. In this tower many of England's great men and women were imprisoned. Many of these have left inscriptions on the walls of this old place. In making of these they beguiled the weary days and months of their imprisonment. Lady Jane Grey has left the word "Jane" upon the walls. On the left of the last recess is a long and interesting inscription, by Charles Bailly, as follows: "The fear of the Lord is the beginning of wisdom." "I.H.S.X.P.S." "Be friend to one—Be ennemye to none." Anno D. 1571, 10 Sept. "The most vnhappy man in the world is he that is not pacient in adversities; For men are not killed with the adversities they have, bvt with ye impacience which they svffer."

"All who come to attend." "The sighs are the true testimonies of my anguish." Act 29th. Charles Bailly. "Hope to the end, and have pacience."

Under Bailly's inscription is one by "ARTHUR POOLE," consisting of the following:—"IHS. A passage perillus makethe a port pleasant. Ao. 1568. Arthur Poole." On the right of the fireplace is the name of John Dudley, Duke of Northumberland, who was confined here in 1533. He carved a device consisting of his family cognizance, "the lion, and bear and ragged staff," underneath which is his name, and the whole is surrounded by a border consisting of oak sprigs, roses, geraniums, and honeysuckles, emblematical of the Christian names of his four brothers, as appears from the unfinished inscription written underneath:

> "Yow that these beasts do wel behold and se,
> May deme with ease wherefore here made they be,
> Withe borders eke wherein
> 4 brothers' names who list to serche the grovnd."

There are many other interesting inscriptions which we can not here reproduce.

Leaving the Beauchamp Tower we visited the

Jewel Tower. This contains the crown jewels and royal regalia, in a circular iron cage. The collection is valued at $20,000,000. The great Kohinoor diamond, now belonging to Victoria, is among the collection. St. Edward's staff is solid gold ornamented with jewels. Here is the baptismal bowl from which kings and queens have been baptized. Queen Victoria's crown consists of a cap of purple velvet, enclosed with hoops of silver, surmounted by a ball on which is a cross. The whole is ornamented with diamonds.

Another place of interest is the famous British Museum. It is midway between Regent's Park and Waterloo Bridge. Under the wings and porticoes of the immense building are Ionic columns. In the entrance hall are beautiful statues and pictures. The collections of antiquities are appropriately arranged and grouped in different rooms of the great buildings. There is an India room and an Egyptian room in which are the collections from ancient Egypt. Its marble statuary is very fine, comprising the Elgin, Phigalean and Townley collections. The library numbers nearly one million volumes. Besides these, there is a large and very important collection of MSS. We saw letters written by Melanchthon, Luther, Sir

Thomas Moore, Drake, Walter Raleigh, Cranmer, Newton, and others. Samples of nearly all of England's sovereigns', statesmen's and authors' chirography are preserved here. The last letter ever penned by Charles Dickens is here also. The collections in natural history are the finest in the the world.

In the centre of the square surrounded by the Museum is the New Reading Room, a hall covered by a large dome of glass. It accommodates four hundred readers or writers. The seats are all numbered, and radiate from the centre like spokes in a wheel. I did not spend much time in the departments which contain the Egyptian Antiquities, inasmuch as I had visited the important and interesting Boulak Museum near Cairo. Here is the celebrated Codex Alexandrinus, which was written A. D. 464, and believed to be the oldest dated MS. of the Bible extant.

The Bank of England is a plain-looking building, but is very large, covering nearly four acres of ground. This bank, besides managing the great debt of England, does an extensive business. Here are gathered the great brokers, stock-jobbers and men handling money for various firms, companies and exchanges.

One afternoon whilst in the city we took a drive in open barouches; the day was delightful. We drove along Pall-Mall, Trafalgar Square, St. James Place and Marlborough, to the house of the Prince of Wales. The home of the Prince of Wales is a large, cool-looking place. But I am sure I have seen as fine homes and residences in America. In St. James' Palace the sovereigns used to reside previous to Victoria's residence in the Buckingham Palace. St. James' Palace has contained the scene of many a birth and many a death. Queen Mary I. and Henry, son of James I., died here. George IV. and James II. were born here. Prince Albert and Queen Victoria were married at St. James, in the chapel. We also drove to Hyde Park, which is one of the finest parks in the world. It covers an area of 500 acres. In it is the beautiful Albert Memorial, erected in 1851 in honor of Prince Albert. At the corners of the elevation on which the monument rests, are groups representing Europe, Asia, Africa, and America. Reliefs and frescoes to the number of 169 occupy the space to the winged angels at the top and on the east and south fronts. The central space contains Prince Albert seated under a grand canopy. Of course we visited Regent's Park, which is nearly as large as

Hyde Park, and just as pretty. It is surrounded by mansions of London's most wealthy people. There are zoölogical and botanical gardens in this park. St. James Park resembles in shape a kite. The head is marked by the Horse Guards in the centre, the Admiralty on the right, the Treasury on the left, and Buckingham palace at the tail. Green Park is famous for its entrance from Piccadilly by a triumphial arch surmounted by a statue of Wellington. It is one of the finest small parks in London.

London has some very fine bridges, among them London Bridge, and Westminster Bridge. The first of these is very old, and figures prominently in story and song. The city has about 1,600 places of worship, and 2,500 including those in suburbs. It has 45 theatres and 400 music halls. The Jews have 25 synagogues. This modern Babylon has 4,500,000 people, but strange to say, of this number only about 30,000 sleep in the city. This is what gives it the deserted appearance on the Sabbath morning, when millions are in their homes in the suburbs. The population is said to increase at the rate of 4,500 annually. London has more Roman Catholics than Rome, more Jews than Palestine, and more Irish than Belfast. Its streets placed end to end would extend from Glasgow to New York. This enormous population and visitors consume 16,000,000 bushels of wheat annually. They eat 800,000 oxen, 4,000,000 sheep, 9,000,000 poultry, and 131,000 tons of fish. The amount of liquids necessary to slake the thirst of this vast population is almost incredible. It is said 150,-000,000 of gallons of water are used daily. In addition to this, 180,000,000 quarts of beer and 31,000,000 quarts of wine are drunk annually.

To move this vast number of people 13,000 cabmen are employed, and the railroads measure 800 miles in the city alone.

Many of the streets are of historical interest. In Charing Cross, not far from the Cockpit, lived Oliver Cromwell, and the poet Spenser died; at Lincoln's Inn Fields, Russell was beheaded. On Tower Hill, some of England's most eminent men were guillotined. Near Whitehall, Charles I. was executed. The writings of Chaucer, Dickens, Fielding and others, have immortalized whole streets and districts. None can walk Fleet street or the Strand without thinking of Johnson, Oliver Goldsmith and Boswell.

In this brief visit it is impossible even to mention half the places of interest. Enough has however been said to convince the reader that of all the cities in Europe, London is one of the most instructive and interesting.

CHAPTER V.

From Brussels to Luzerne—The Country and the Houses—Luzerne—Lake—Bridges—Cathedral—The Lion—Rigi and Pilatus—Luzerne to Milan—Grand Sceneries—St. Gothard—Into Italy—Change of Scenery.

ON the twenty-fifth of January, before it was daylight, we were on our way to the railway depot. At that hour already we met many peasants who had come from the country with their dog-carts loaded with vegetables for the markets of Brussels. By daylight we were in an express train bound for Luzerne. We went by way of Strassburg, Metz and Basel, a distance of 500 miles over the "Central Railroad of Belgium," "Wilhelm, Luxembourg and Alsace-Lorraine," and "Switzerland" railroads. These roads take the traveler through well-cultivated districts in Belgium, Germany and Switzerland. The wagon roads everywhere are piked and well kept. The houses of the peasants are constructed of stone. The stable occupies the ground floor, or the one end of what otherwise look like comfortable homes. The manure pile before the front door is a substitute for serpentine walks and choice flower plots in our country. Here for the first time I saw women carrying immense bundles of wood on their heads. They wear great wooden shoes, short skirts, and generally have bare heads. Notwithstanding their life of drudgery and their apparently uncomfortable clothing, they seem content and happy. We had a pleasant all-day journey, with a good warm lunch neatly packed in a little basket.

At eight o'clock we arrived in Luzerne, very tired and very hungry. We were soon around a bounteous dinner table in the large and beautiful hotel "Sweitzerhof." Early the next day we were ready to see the beautiful town. Luzerne is on both sides of a crystal lake of the same name. This lake is four miles long, and for the most part twelve hundred feet deep. The town receives its name from the light-house which stood here many years ago to guide boatmen on the lake and river Reuss. It has a wall on the land side which dates its beginning to feudal times. Three old bridges span the river, the oldest of which was built at the beginning of the fourteenth century. This bridge contains seventy-five pictures illustrative of Swiss history. The Muhlenbrücke, built in 1625, has a series of paintings called the "Dance of Death."

SCENERY ON LAKE LUZERNE.

The pictures represent human beings engaged in almost every work and pastime from the cradle to the grave. In every one of these scenes is a picture of death. The Cathedral is a large building, and is noted for its organ, which is said to be the finest in the world.

In the northern part of the town is a high rock into which is cut the figure of a lion dying upon a shield, in commemoration of the death of the Swiss guards who died in defence of the Tuileries, August 10th, 1792. The model was designed by Thorwaldsen.

Standing upon the shore of Lake Luzerne one has a splendid view of Mount Rigi, ten miles away. The grand old mountain is clad in a garment of eternal white. Close to the town is Pilatus, towering to the height of 7000 foet. This is the mount, tradition says, which Pilate touched with his feet when he was borne by invisible hands from Jerusalem after delivering Christ to be crucified. Two springs of pure water mark the spot where his feet touched. A hotel is situated near the springs. It must be a delightful spot, up there among the clouds where the scorching heat is never felt. Of course nobody believes the tradition. After visiting the shores and making a thorough tour of the old town, we were again on the wing.

From Luzerne to Milan in Italy the scenery is sublime. For the first ten miles after leaving Luzerne the traveler passes through a well cultivated country. There are pleasant homes, large apple orchards, and plenty of wood on the hillsides. After passing Lake Zug we begin to enter a veritable wonderland. There in the distance is old Rigi with its snow-capped summit looking like a mountain of burnished silver! The train passes rapidly onward. The scenery changes. Slowly, majestically, the great mountains come into view. The clouds hover along the sides of these great giant peaks, half way up their naked outlines, as if nature tried to cast a drapery around her grand handiwork, lest the soul of the beholder be ravished with the sublimity of the scene. The glistening snows and ice on those mighty summits are the resplendent light-houses lighting the soul heavenward from nature to nature's God. What mean those rapturous heart-throbs as she beholds these sublime scenes! Does not the soul by thus beating against its fetters of clay teach that she is destined to be free, to soar higher than these sublime peaks to a world more perfect in loveliness, and more pure because unstained by sin? A short distance from Brunnen a great rock more than one hundred feet high shoots out of the water as if pushed upward by a mighty giant. This is called "Schillerstein." After passing this natural monument the traveler enters St. Gothard's pass. The ascent is gradual. Erst Feld station is surrounded by peaks sheer up a thousand feet.

> "Round *their* breasts the rolling clouds are spread,
> Eternal sunshine settles on *their* head."

People build huge stone fences to keep the sliding earth and snows from crushing their growing crops and obliterating their little homes. In the ravines the railroad engineers have erected huge walls of solid masonry to prevent the rocks from tumbling on the tracks. We now pass through one tunnel after another; soon there are railroads far above and far beneath us. Over those above we will soon pass; over those below we have just come. We go up, up, until we are 7000 feet above the level of the sea. The ascent has been so gradual, so quiet, and the air so clear, the scenery so sublime that the ride is voted the grandest of our lives. God built in St. Gothard a mighty monument, and Mr. Brunell, the engineer of this railroad, has carved the inscription of what man can do in this great achievement. I saw on the summit of the mountain near the restaurant a sample of American enterprise. In white letters upon a great rock, a countryman has written, "USE AMERICAN CHOCOLATE-DROPS."

We took our lunch in cloud-land, in a restaurant built up there. The table was well supplied with everything calculated to satisfy a hungry man's appetite. The sides of the room of the restaurant are ornamented with large lettered mottoes. The following are some of them: "Trank und Speis starkt zur Reis," "Aufrechtigkeit ist die beste List," "First think, then drink."

Before we speak of the descent it is well to note that St. Gothard's tunnel is nine and a quarter miles long, which is 2930 yards longer than Mt. Cenis. Express trains pass through it in twenty minutes. It was opened May 22, 1882, after working upon it ten years. The average number of men employed was 2500. At times as high as 3400 were at work. The line has fifty-six tunnels, twenty-five and a half miles long. It also has thirty-two large and twenty-four smaller bridges, and ten viaducts. The work cost $11,-000,000.

Soon after lunch we heard "All aboard!" and then we went toward Italy. The descent begins; soon we look down into little valleys—

"Through the parting clouds only
The earth can be seen,
Far down neath the vapor
The meadow of green."

Soon we are on the borders of sunny Italy. We pass the lakes Lugano and Maggiore, with their magnificent sceneries. We have come to the edge of Como, with its precipitous mountain banks two or three thousand feet high. Along the shore are handsome mansions, the summer residences of the wealthy. We feel that we have come to summer-land. The weather is pleasantly warm. It begins to rain. This causes the Italians along the road to put on their overcoats. With their hoods drawn over their heads, their dark features look quite savage. The houses we now see are stone, like those elsewhere; but they have a neglected air, which contrasts strangely with the beautiful valleys and hillsides with which the flying train has displaced the deep ravines and towering cliffs. We realize that we are in a Roman Catholic country. There are numerous shrines along the road, before which pious Catholics bow for a moment's prayer. There are acres of vines which in the summer are laden with luscious grapes. Finally darkness closes upon the scene. After passing a number of towns in the darkness, we at length enter a large depot. We have arrived at Milan. After some delay, occasioned by a desire of the officious custom-house officers to review our baggage, which had already been done when we entered Italy, we were permitted to proceed on our way to the hotel. A good dinner at ten o'clock, a short walk afterwards, and I was off to bed.

CHAPTER VI.

PARIS—Situation and Size—Boulevards—Catacombs—Bois de Boulogne—Madeleine—Louvre--Palais Royal—Hotel des Invalides—Tomb of Napoleon—Cathedral—La St. Chapelle—Pantheon—St. Jacques—Bourse—Place de la Concorde.
VERSAILLES—Location—Royal Palace—Rooms of Marie Antoinette—Mirror--Museum--Paintings--Gardens—Lyons—Manufactures—Cathedral—Marseilles—Quays—Streets—Cathedral—Rain and the President.

PARIS is the second city in Europe in point of size, and the first in beauty. Its population is about one-half of that of London. It is situated in the centre of northern France. It is an old city, and formed a part of Cæsar's dominion, B. C. 56. It was small then, having an area of only thirty-seven acres. At present its area is more than 20,000 acres, or thirty square miles. The city is surrounded by a wall broken by 57 gates, besides the numerous entrances of the railroads. Paris is surrounded by low hills which are almost entirely covered by flower gardens, from which come the beautiful flowers which fill the great markets and decorate the thousands of homes and churches. Immediately inside of the defences is one of the great boulevards called the Military street. This street entirely surrounds Paris and is known under different names in different parts of its course. Another set of boulevards forms a circle around the centre of the city. When Louis Philippe was on the throne the city was greatly improved. It was then these boulevards were laid out where the old city ramparts once stood. These streets are the finest in Paris, and are filled from morning until late at night with persons bent on shopping and sight-seeing. That which makes these streets so beautiful is their width, their green trees, and their magnificent buildings of light stone. This stone is nearly as white as marble. Much of it was taken from quarries which existed over one-eighth of the area beneath the city. It is estimated that 324,-000,000 cubic feet of stone have been taken out of these now exhausted quarries. The stone when first brought to the light of day is so soft that it can be cut with a plane. The ornamentation is done after the stones are in position in the wall.

One of the most beautiful drives in the world is through the Bois de Boulogne. This is the principal park in Paris. The most fashionable entrance is along the Champs Elysees. This park is nearly three times as large as Central Park. It has beautiful flower-beds, elegant walks, large handsome trees, an immense aquarium, and many other attractions. The principal avenue is one hundred yards wide and extends a distance of ten miles. All along this beautiful avenue are side walks for pedestrians, a road for horseback riding, and a carriage drive. There are other parks in and near Paris but the only fine exterior one besides the Bois de Boulogne is the Bois de Vincennes. Many of the squares throughout the city have small parks.

To describe all the places of interest on this magnificent city is beyond the province of this volume. We will visit some of those which are most famous. The finest specimen of Greek architecture in the world is the Madeleine (St. Mary Magdalene). It is a hundred and fifty feet broad and a hundred feet high. It is surrounded by a line of fifty-two Corinthian columns, forty-nine feet high. The church has bronze doors over thirty feet high. They are covered with Old Testament scenes illustrating the Ten Commandments. Over the front pillars on the pediment is a scene of the Judgment which is indeed beautiful as a work of art, and impressive, inasmuch as it illustrates one of the most awful scenes of which Revelation speaks. The sides within and the floors are of the finest marble. There are grand pieces of sculpture in this church. There were two weddings in progress when I was in this magnificent building. The scene was quite different from what it was in 1871, when upwards of 300 insurgents who had sought refuge here were put to the sword.

One of the most interesting places in this city is the Louvre. This is the depository of vast treasures of art. It was begun in 1541, and was formerly the residence of the kings of France. "The collections in the Louvre comprise Assyrian antiquities, Egyptian antiquities, Algerian discoveries, sculptures of the Renaissance, modern sculptures, marble antiques, paintings of the Italian school, paintings of the Spanish school, paintings of the German school, paintings of the Flemish school, paintings of the Dutch school, museum of jewelery, museum of Hebrew antiquities, museum of the Kings, museum of Mediæval art, museum of Designs, museum of the Navy, museum of Ethnography, and American museum."

Here are the sword of Napoleon I., with its diamond handle, and two crowns adorned with diamonds and precious stones. It was only last summer that a large diamond shown at the Paris

Exhibition was purchased and added to this collection. In this collection are many of the gems and crystal ware, once the property of royalty. One is impressed with the fact that the possession of all this wealth and splendor is but transient. Those who once prized these treasures as their own personal property are gone to the land where wealth of this world has no power.

Besides the almost innumerable paintings and the crown jewels, there is a museum of Egyptian antiquities, illustrating the domestic and the religious life of these ancient people. One can almost imagine himself in the Boulak Museum as he goes from one object of interest to the other in this stupendous collection. There is likewise an Assyrian collection, which gives one an excellent idea of this ancient civilization.

It must be admitted that the collection of sculpture is not as fine as that of Florence or that in the Vatican, but it is by no means to be despised. The famous Venus of Milo is in a room by itself. The figure is armless, but the expression of the face, the graceful attitude and the life-like form, make up this deficiency. We cannot give even an idea of all to be seen in these vast halls and saloons of magnificence. Neither could a study of months fully master a history of these paintings, nor enter into the spirit of genius displayed on every side. These works are many of them the product of genius tinctured by feeling wrought by the events of the times.

The new opera house is the finest in the world. It covers nearly three acres of ground. The entrances are through sculptured arches. The interior is magnificent, with its statuary, its mosaics, and reliefs. The grand staircase consists of white marble steps, with balustrades and hand-rails of precious stones. Fifty people can stand abreast on one of the steps below the division. The stage is nearly two hundred feet long and seventy-five feet deep. There is a huge mirror at the end of the lobby which makes the building appear of unlimited length. The grandeur of this great playhouse can scarcely be appreciated, even when seen: much less can it be described.

The Palais Royal is frequented by visitors to Paris. The elegance of its jewelry stores, the splendor of its restaurants, and the many people wandering through and along its beautiful avenues, make it a place worthy of many visits. This palace was built by Cardinal Richelieu. He died in 1642. From that time until the Commune in

1871 it was occupied by royalty and members of the royal family. This magnificent pile of buildings suffered not a little at the hands of the Revolutionists in 1848. There is a small cannon which is so arranged that the rays of the sun are concentrated about the fuse with sufficient power to fire it off, thus telling the Parisians when it is high noon.

After having taken a drive to the Exposition buildings and viewed the grounds and the famous Eiffel tower, we visited the Hotel des Invalides. This magnificent soldiers' home was begun by Louis XIV., and finished in 1674. "In the gardens is a battery of artillery called the 'Triumphal Battery,' composed of guns taken in the wars of the First Empire, in the Crimea, in Algeria, and in China. Above the entrance to the building appears a fine bas-relief representing Louis XIV. on horseback, with Justice and Prudence. Behind the façade are five Courts of Honor, and arcades containing mural paintings illustrative of the military glories of France; a statue of Napoleon I.; and the Museum of Artillery. The dining-halls, kitchens and dormitories of the pensioners may be visited, as well as the Council Chamber (portrait of Napoleon I.) and library of 60,000 volumes."*

---

*Official Guide.

The last soldier who fought under Napoleon I. died two years ago.

The church adjoining the soldiers' home is worthy of notice. It at one time contained all the battle-flags taken in the wars of Napoleon I., to the number of 3,000. It has a magnificent painting of Christ in the tomb. But what distinguishes it most is the tomb of Napoleon I. In the central part of the church is this magnificent tomb, where the body of Napoleon I. rests since 1840, when it was brought from St. Helena. The church itself is a square building 198 feet in breadth. It is surmounted by a dome 344 feet high; this dome is 86 feet in diameter. Immediately beneath this dome is the crypt, in the form of a basin, with walls of polished granite. In the centre of this basin is a sarcophagus of Finland granite. This rests upon a block of green granite. The gallery which surrounds the crypt is ornamented with bas-reliefs illustrating the achievements of the great man. Twelve statues under this gallery and around the sarcophagus represent the warrior's twelve principal victories. Here there repose the ashes of the man who once made tyrants tremble. At his hand his countrymen suffered much and gained much. If he was a whip of scorpions in the hands of the

Almighty, his chastisements were attended with many reformations. He was ambitious, but

> "Who knows but He whose hand the lightning forms,
> Who heaves old ocean, and who wings the storms,
> Pours fierce ambition in a Cæsar's mind?"

Charity says "*Requiescat in pace!*"

The chapel of Louis XIV. is noted for its beautiful stained-glass windows of the eleventh century. We have already spoken of the Madeleine, but this is only one of the many churches of Paris. The cathedral of Notre Dame stands on the spot which was occupied by a Roman temple. A church, dedicated to St. Stephen, stood here as early as 360. The first stone of the present edifice was laid three and a quarter centuries before America was discovered. The glass stained windows are famous, especially the "Catherine Whell" window on the north front. The carvings, columns and arches in the building are very pretty. The organ is one of the finest in the world. In this church are a "part of the true cross and crown of thorns" brought from Palestine by St. Louis. On the one tower is a bell brought from Sebastopol, on the other is the great Bourdon, one of the largest bells in the world. There are many awaiting the archangel's trump at the resurrection morn in the large vaults beneath. When I was there the priests were chanting mass at a coffin about to be placed with the great majority.

Here is a painting illustrative of the dream of the wife of Prince Harcourt. She dreamed that her husband was buried before he was dead. She had him exhumed, and found her dream true. There is an angel representing marriage and a man coming out of the tomb before the Duchess in kneeling posture.

Near by the Cathedral rises the arrow-like spire of *La Saint Chapelle*. This church was built in three years (1245–8) by St. Louis, to receive the part of the true cross and crown of thorns which are now in Notre Dame. For many years this church lay in partial ruin, but it was thoroughly restored from 1837 to 1867. "It now presents the completest, perhaps the finest, specimen of religious architecture of the thirteenth century."

The Pantheon (or St. Genevieve's) is in the form of a Greek cross. The four aisles unite under a dome 66 feet in diameter and 258 feet high. Madame Pompadour was the instigator of the building of this church, to replace an edifice which had been dedicated to St. Genevieve, the patron saint of the city. It was made a church in 1822, became a Pantheon again in 1831, and in 1853 it again became a church. In 1848 the interior was damaged by cannon-shots fired at the insurgents who had taken refuge there. The Communists were about to visit a worse fate upon it in 1871. They had already stored gunpowder and petroleum in it with which to blow it up, but they were driven out before their nefarious work could be accomplished. The crypt contains tombs of some of those who with Madame Pompadour helped to plunge the French people into sin and infidelity.

There is a beautiful painting illustrating scenes in the life of Joan d'Arc in this building. The first scene represents her as a shepherdess receiving inspiration from an angel, who is in the attitude of whispering into her ear. The next scene represents her with sword in hand leading the army to victory. Again she stands behind the king as he is crowned. A smile of peace lights up her countenance. The last scene represents her kissing the cross when she is already tied to the stake. We went all through the crypts beneath the church. They are marvels of solid masonry. We next visited the Palais du Luxembourg. The building dates from 1615. It has been the residence of princes, a prison in the Revolution, Chamber of Peers in the time of Louis Philippe, a senate house, etc. Now it contains paintings from the great French painters now living and a hall adorned with beautiful statuary. The ceiling of the gallery is adorned with paintings representing the Zodiac. The chapel adjoining is of the sixteenth century.

On the Rue de Rivoli stands the tower of St. Jacques. The church was pulled down by the revolutionists. It is centrally located, and affords from its top a fine view of the city. The bridges over the Seine, the windings of the river, the parks and the great buildings, lie as on a map at your feet.

We saw the Morgue, the dead house where unidentified persons found in the city limits are brought. There was rather a hard-looking crowd standing about the doors and in the narrow room in which, separated from the crowd of visitors by a glass casing, the dead are exposed to view. Here on a chair, as if ready to be shaved, a poor rather debauched body reclined. As soon as they are identified the bodies are covered and then removed. If they are not identified within three days they are interred at the public expense. We visited the Bourse, or stock exchange. The building has been compared with the Temple of Vespasian in the Forum at Rome. The inside is surrounded by a gallery from which a good view is had of the shrieking "bulls and bears" in the vast room beneath. Here it is that fortunes are made and lost. Many have gone there light-hearted and have come away in despair. Stock gambling in Paris and everywhere else should be branded as what it really is, a lottery and a crime.

Between the Jardin des Tuileries and the Champs Elysees is the famous Place de la Concorde. It is the finest square in any city in Europe, if not in the world. "In the centre stands the Obelisk of Luxor, a monolith of red granite, 72 feet high, brought from the ruins of Thebes, and erected in 1836. It is a sister of Cleopatra's Needle, and was presented to the French Government by Mehemet Ali; the cost of bringing it from Egypt was two million francs. A person standing close to the Obelisk can see the Arc de Triomphe, the Madeleine, the Louvre, the Chambre des Députés, and other public buildings. On the north and south sides are fine fountains, adorned with tritons, nereides, and various allegorical statues; one of the fountains represents River Navigation and the other Sea Navigation. The actual *Place* is bounded by eight colossal statues typical of the chief towns of France, namely: Lyons, Marseilles, Bordeaux, Nantes, Rouen, Brest, Lille, and Strasburg. The last-named town was lost to France in 1870, but the statue is cherished and visited on National Fête Day by crowds of Alsatian-Lorraines, who literally cover it with immortelles to the memory of those who fell in the great battles fought in the annexed provinces." *

In this square more blood has been shed and more awful scenes have been enacted than upon any piece of ground of its size in the world. When Marie Antoinette and Louis XVI. were married, they discharged fireworks on this great square, when a panic ensued, in which no less than 1000 persons were killed, and many more were injured. Here began the conflict between royalty and the people which resulted in the destruction of the Bastile. Here nearly 3000 people in less than a year and a half were beheaded. Among them were the King and Marie Antoinette, Charlotte Corday, ⸲Danton, Robespierre, and others who were great in "that strange spell, a name." Some

---

* Official Guide.

of them were good and innocent. At night the myriads of gas-lights give the whole scene a splendor which must be seen to be appreciated. The great revolving light in the Eiffel tower, beheld from this square, looks like a beautiful ever changing star as it flashes in contrast, and far down the brilliant scene in the square. I can not in this little volume speak of Paris churches, clubs, columns and conservatories, of its fortifications, its fountains, its fine houses, homes, hotels, its markets, its museums, its towers and its people. Suffice to say it has every splendor and beauty to make it merit its name, "Beautiful Paris." It has conveniences for rich and poor as no other city has; but then it has its hideous vices and its many crimes to justly entitle it to the opproprious name of "Wicked Paris."

Everybody who visits Paris should also see Versailles. The drive to this historic town is very pretty. The road passes by the Mongso Park, which in the spring and summer is very beautiful. Further on the tourist passes the little historic town of St. Cloud where Marie Antoinette once resided, and in later years, was the home of Napoleon First. During the Franco-Prussian war the French themselves destroyed the palace.

It was a wet, cold morning in April when I wished to go to Versailles, so to save time and avoid the rain I took the train at Saint-Lazare. We rode on top of the cars, which are especially arranged for the conveninence of tourists.

Versailles was once a city of one hundred and fifty thousand or more people; now the population does not reach one-third that number. The streets are beautifully laid out with mathematical precision. The principal and only real attraction is the royal palace.

The palace is built in a hollow square, with the side toward the city open. Here is the courtyard, adorned with sixteen statutes taken from the bridge *La Concorde* in Paris. They represent sixteen of France's great warriors. The palace itself was originally a hunting lodge. It is said a mill was here located, and that Louis XIII. took refuge in it during a shower of rain. He was pleased with the location so he built a hunter's lodge. Louis XIV. determined to make it the most beautiful royal residence in the world. After working upon it twelve years, and expending $200,000,000 upon it, the monarch moved into it in 1670. He lived in it forty-five years. In one of the rooms the old king used to sit by the window, and when a carriage of state entered containing any one the monarch did not wish to see, he would hide in a closet near by. Here he would conceal himself to listen to what his courtiers said of him. I stood by the window where Louis XIV. sat when he died. There is a picture in tapestry of this monarch in the palace, upon which the artist worked fourteen years, and which cost a fortune. It was in one of the rooms of this palace that Marie Antoinette heard the fiends come to drag her to prison. She escaped by a secret stairway in her night-clothes (October 5, 1789), only to be apprehended a few days afterwards. Her Swiss guards, faithful to the end, perished in their attempt to defend their mistress. She died four years and eleven days after that eventful night, on the guillotine. In one of this beautiful queen's rooms is a mirror which when one stands in a certain position, shows the body without a head. It is said as soon as the queen saw this mirror she said it was a prophecy of the death she would eventually die. The room in which Peter the Great slept in 1777 is very prettily furnished, the bed on which he reposed is still to be seen. After the death of Louis XVI., this grand palace remained unoccupied for many years. Louis

Philippe converted it into a vast museum of all "the glories" of France. There are whole acres of canvas in the many rooms, some of the paintings having been specially made for the place. In the historical museum there are eleven rooms filled with paintings, illustrating the history of France from the year 511 to Louis XIV. in 1700. Besides these there are many rooms illustrating the more modern history of France, and besides these there are ten rooms illustrating chiefly the military glories of Napoleon and the First Empire. Then, too, there is the *Galerie de l'Empire*, consisting of fourteen rooms, illustrating the campaigns from the year 1796 to 1810. Besides all these, there are rooms filled with portraits.

The chapel in the palace is the place where royalty worshiped. It is very pretty. Its organ is one of the finest in Europe. In this chapel Louis XVI. and Marie Antoinette were married. The frescoing on the ceiling is very fine. An angel's limb is so frescoed that it seems pending. The deception is complete. The theatre, once the place where wealth and beauty assembled, is seldom used now. It was here the Garde du Corps assembled at the memorable banquet of 1789. Here, too, the Queen of England banqueted August 25, 1855.

The grounds surrounding the palace are in keeping with the magnificence within. There are beautiful fountains, artificial lakes, and serpentine walks.

There are three principal divisions of the Gardens—the Parterre d'Eau, facing the centre of the Palace, the Parterre du Nord, facing the north wing, and the Parterre du Midi, facing the south wing of the Palace. The Parterre d'Eau possesses two basins, with fountains rising in the form of a basket. Twenty-four bronze statues surround these, typifying the chief rivers of France, and eight statues of water-nymphs and eight groups of children complete the environment. The terrace is flanked by two grand fountains, the Fontaine de Diane, on the right, the Fontaine du Point Jour, on the left; they are adorned with groups of animals fighting.

The traveler, in passing from Paris to Marseilles, has a view of the country which in many places is of interest, but there is nothing striking about it, so as to make a description of the rural scenery of special importance. A little more than half way between Paris and Marseilles is Lyons. It is situated at the junction of the Saone and Rhone, and is the largest manufacturing city in France. Many of the houses in the older part of the city are seven to nine stories high. Where the streets are narrow and crooked, the light of day has difficulty in finding its way to the ground between these high buildings. There are, however, some very fine streets with beautiful houses in the city. There are over fifty squares in the town. A few of them are very fine. Lyons produces the finest silks in the world. There are manufactories of cotton and woolen goods, hats, chemicals, drugs, liquors and earthenware. Next to Paris, it excels all other European cities in the manufacture of sham jewelry. It has fine quays at the junctions of the two rivers.

There are few buildings worthy of note in this city. The Hotel de Ville or City Hall is finer than that in Paris. The opera house and Palais St. Pierre, once a convent, now an institute for science and literature, and museum of sculpture, archæology and natural history, are on the great square called the Terreaux. The Cathedral, Notre Dame de Fourvières, dates its beginning to the ninth century. It is called de Fourvières because it is said to stand on the site of an old Roman forum. It has a figure of the Virgin on the top of the tower, 400 feet above the street below.

The distance from Lyons to Marseilles is 175 miles. This is the great seaport of France. Upon its streets may be seen people from every part of the world. An extensive trade is carried on by this city with all Mediterranean ports. The harbor of Marseilles is very fine. The town is protected by three fortified islands, having light-houses to guide the many vessels which pass between these islands on their way to the harbor. Outside of the city are the great docks, having warehouses which cover nearly a hundred acres. Altogether, the harbor of the city has an area of nearly 500 acres and over four miles of dockage. In summer-time the people seek relief from the oppressive heat in boats on the bay.

Many of the streets of the city are wide, clean, and well-paved. Large stone structures, in which are the principal business places, line these thoroughfares. When I was in Marseilles, the streets were decorated with flags and buntings and greens in honor of the newly-elected President, who was then on a tour through the principal cities of France. The holiday attire and the grand processions may have enhanced the beauty of the city, but notwithstanding, Marseilles is a pretty town at all times.

Of course Marseilles has a Cathedral. It stands where the Massilian citadel stood when it was besieged by Cæsar. Before the citadel occupied the place, a temple of Diana was there; and before that, an altar dedicated to Baal. Near the port is the Bourse, with a Corinthian portico. The interior is very handsome, and is conceded to be finer than the Bourse at Paris. The Chamber of Commerce is decorated with paintings and gildings. It is the finest room in the building. The Palace of Arts was built about twenty years ago. It has two wings and three towers. The centre tower is the largest, and beautifully ornamented with statuary. Immediately below this tower is a fountain from which the water spouts high into the air. On account of the rain, which fell in great torrents when we were in this beautiful seaport, our sight-seeing was cut short. It was the first European city we saw after returning from Palestine. There were few Arabs to be seen—most of the few we had brought with us as steerage passengers on the "Gerunda." To be among Europeans, and not to see everywhere a crowd of turbaned, half-naked men, pushing and jostling each other, and calling for *backsheash*, was in itself a relief. We could appreciate our brief stay in Marseilles, notwithstanding the rain.

MILAN CATHEDRAL.

CHAPTER VII.

Milan, Age—Cathedral—Spire—Nail of "True Cross"—Tomb of Borromeo—St. Ambrose—The "Brazen Serpent"—The Last Supper, by Da Vinci—Other Buildings — Florence— Scenery on Way, etc.—Pitti Palace and Palace Vecchio— Duomo—Campanile—Santa Croce—Amerigo Vespucci.

MILAN is an ancient city. It was old already when Christ was born. In the twelfth century, Frederic Barbarossa nearly entirely destroyed it, but it was soon rebuilt. It has been besieged many times in the centuries which have elapsed since its foundations were laid. In 1576, it was desolated by the plague. It has recovered from all its misfortunes, and to-day it is the cleanest and most prosperous city in Italy. Some streets are narrow and winding, but they are well paved and clean.

The great centre of attraction in Milan is the Cathedral. It was begun in 1387, and is unfinished to this day. In fret-work, carving and statuary, it is said to excel all other churches in the world. It is the second largest church in Europe. The inside measurements are 477 feet by 183 feet. The tower rises to the height of 360 feet. We ascended to the roof before breakfast. We went up by 200 marble steps. It is quite an undertaking before the morning meal. From the roof we had a grand view of the city and the distant mountains. From the tower the view is superb. On the roof the tourist is surrounded by a world of beauty. It is adorned with ninety Gothic turrets. Mont Blanc and Monte Rosa can be distinctly seen, whilst far beyond them towers the Matterhorn with its ice-covered summits, like peaks of silver in the morning sunlight. The exterior of the building is white marble. In the niches and on the pinnacle there is room for 4500 statues, of which about 3500 are in position. Nearly everybody who is of any note in the Bible or in Italian and Christian history has a statue on this cathedral. The wealth of beauty is perfectly bewildering. The whole exterior in fact is so vast, yet so delicate and beautiful is the work, that one feels that it is too nice to be out of doors. Within, the floor is in mosaic of red, blue and white marble. Fifty-two pillars, eighty feet high, support the roof. In the nave, marked by a light which glistens like a diamond far above the floor, the visitor is shown "a nail of the true cross."

More wonderful than this is the tomb of St. Carlo Borromeo, in a crypt beneath the high altar. The body reposes in a marble tomb, the whole front of which is moved by machinery. Inside the marble is a glass case which contains the body. It is shrunken by age, but the features are well preserved. Jewels and precious stones of every description, to the value of more than a million dollars, have been heaped upon the corpse by those who have come here to worship from every part of the world. As I gazed upon this wealth I could not help thinking that if he were able, the man who in his life had given his personal fortune and even the works of art and the ornaments of his palace for the relief of the poor, would certainly not tolerate this idolatry. He would speedily turn the useless wealth on his ashes into bread for those who go hungry under the very shadow of the cathedral towers.

The traveler is loth to leave the interior of this majestic building. The fifty-two marble pillars which support the roof are ninety feet in height. Its noble and costly altars, its grand old Gothic arches, its matchless stained-glass windows, its historic tombs, and even its worn floors, impress the soul and fill it with indescribable emotions.

Another quite remarkable church in Milan is that of St. Ambrose. It is built on the site of an ancient temple dedicated to Bacchus. The doors are covered with chiseled bronze, which was on the doors through which Theodosius wished to pass (in the fourth century) after he returned from the massacre at Thessalonica. St. Ambrose, whose name the church bears, was born at Treves in Gaul, in A. D. 340, and died here in 397. He is interred in this church. Here he preached, and in this city he labored until the Master took him from the Church militant to the Church triumphant. The pulpit from which he used to preach is still shown here. So also are some of the letters penned by his hand. There is an illuminated MS. of the *Te laudamus* written for him. In this church the tomb of Pepin, father of Charlemagne, is located. There are frescoes on the wall of the second and third centuries. The visitor is shown a column surmounted by a serpent said to be the "brazen serpent" which Moses raised in the wilderness. It cannot speak for itself, and there is no mark upon it to establish its identity, so I cannot say whether the legend with regard to it is true or not. It certainly is *very old*. The refectory of the ancient Dominican convent, now the church of

Santa Maria delle Grazie, contains the celebrated fresco of the "Last Supper," by Leonardo da Vinci. Although blackened by age and defaced by those who knew not how to appreciate it, it still shows the inspiration and skill of the master hand that placed it there. It alone is worth a visit to Milan. It is said Milan has charities which possess upwards of $40,000,000 of property. There is a hospital here founded in the fifteenth century which is nearly 1000 feet long and 360 feet in depth. The treasury, the palace of justice, the palace of science, the mint, and the public loan bank, are all fine buildings. The railroad depots here, as in other Italian cities, contain fine frescoes. There are also fine stores in Milan. The "Galleria Vittorio Emanuele" is the great centre around which whole armies of shoppers, both from the city and from other places, hover entranced, I may say, by the pretty wares of every description. It is an immense arcade; the roof is glass, and at one place, 180 feet above the marble floor. The building is lighted by a myriad of gas-jets, giving the whole an appearance of brilliancy, wealth and gayety which must be seen to be appreciated. The people of Milan are the finest and most polite in all Italy.

From Milan we took the noon train for Florence. It is 216 miles by rail from Milan to Florence. In Switzerland we were in a climate as cold as at home; now it is warm as May. The trees are in blossom, although it is the 27th of February. The country south of Milan is beautiful and very fertile. Every foot is historical, some of the most momentous events in Roman history having transpired here. We cross high, long bridges, but there is no water. The channel is dry. When the snows on the mountains melt, these dry channels are filled to overflowing. The buildings in the country and the small towns, look, as they really are, very old. The cattle in the fields are large and in good condition. The carriage roads here, as elsewhere in Europe, are nicely graded and in good repair. Several hours before we arrive in Florence we cross the Apennines. The scenery is not near so grand as in the Alps, although there are some very pretty views. Tunnels are numerous and built of the most enduring masonry.

It was some time after the shadows of night had enveloped the quiet valleys when we arrived at Florence. After a ten o'clock dinner we took a little stroll and then retired. We stop at the hotel

FLORENCE.

Washington. The Arno flows on the other side of the street. The outlook is pretty in the extreme. Many of the hotels in Italian cities are old palaces once inhabited by princes. We had arisen early, and after a breakfast of eggs, rolls and chocolate, we went sight-seeing. The chief beauty of Florence is not in fine buildings, although some are very grand; it lies in her priceless treasures of art. The principal depositories of art are the Pitti Palace and the Palace Vecchio, the old capital of the republic and afterwards the home of Cosmo. It is public property now. The foundations of the building were laid two centuries before America was discovered. The Pitti Palace contains the finest paintings in Europe. Here are the original masterpieces from which copies and chromos are made and sent through the world. They are the works of Michael Angelo, Murillo, Rubens, and other masters. The Pitti Palace and Palace Vecchio are connected by a bridge over the Arno. This is in itself a storehouse of art. Among the statues in the room called the Tribune in the Uffizi Gallery, are the Dancing Faun, the famous Venus de Medici, seventeen centuries old. Another room contains jewels valued at $20,000,000. The most beautiful ware of rock crystal adorns the cases.

In another room is a table of Florentine mosaics valued at $150,000. It took fourteen people twenty-five years to make it. There is another in another room which cost $200,000, and fifteen years were consumed in its manufacture.

As I looked on these treasures I could not help thinking of those who once called them their own. Where are the spirits of those who once feasted their eyes upon these gems, and the hands that once held these costly wares? Here their souls were filled with anxieties and fears of which we can form no estimate. Once the beauty of their bodies was enhanced by these glittering gems. Do crowns imperishable rest upon their brows in the other world? These rooms have much to tell us of wealth and beauty, of kings and sceptres. We may well say, "Can wealth give happiness?" Look round and see.

What gay distress, what splendid misery, these gems and paintings commemorate! But I have not told you half. One gallery has a series of busts of Roman emperors. Another has portraits of the most famous painters, executed for the most part by themselves. To describe all that is contained in these galleries would require a volume larger than this one.

Florence has 172 churches, not a few of which are large and beautiful structures. Of these the Duomo or Cathedral is the largest, and in architectural grandeur is surpassed only by St. Peter's at Rome. It was begun in 1294, and was not completed until the middle of the last century. Black, red and white marble in variegated figures covers the sides. The dome of this church (which is the largest in the world) served Michael Angelo as a model for St. Peter's. Among the statues in the church the unfinished group representing the entombment of Christ, by Michael Angelo, is the most famous.

The Campanile or belfry near the Cathedral is 550 years old, and is an elegant sample of Italian Gothic style of architecture. Charles V. used to say of this what Napoleon I. said of the tower of the Antwerp Cathedral—it deserved to be put beneath a glass case. To my eyes the one at Antwerp far excels the former. In 1604, Ferdinand I., grand-duke of Tuscany, began a mausoleum for his family. It is not finished yet, but it has already cost $17,000,000. It is an octagon ninety-four feet in diameter and two hundred feet high, and is lined with lapis lazuli, jasper, onyx, and other precious stones. The acoustic properties of this mausoleum are wonderful. Standing along the wall and singing the scale produces the sweetest music, echoed and re-echoed from the sides and dome.

The church of Santa Croce is the Westminster Abbey of Florence. It contains the tomb of that greatest of painters and sculptors the modern world has produced, the immortal Angelo. There too repose the ashes of Galileo, the great astronomer, and Leonardo Aretino, the greatest Italian writer of the fifteenth century. Here too is the splendid monument of Dante, but his ashes are at Ravenna. Not far from the banks of the Arno the old home of Amerigo Vespucci is still to be seen. Not far from the home once owned by the man after whom America was named is the old mansion of Dante. The houses, although renewed and repaired, show the marks of great age. Galileo lived on the hillside from which he could overlook the city and sweep the skies with his rude telescope, which disclosed to his astonished gaze the individual, sparkling mosaics in that grand pavement of light, the Milky Way.

In this city, close to the Palazzo Vecchio, is the fountain of Neptune and Triton, on the very spot where in May, 1498, Savonarola was burnt at the stake. On that day a fierce mob clamored for his death as he was led out from his prison, but for two hundred and fifty years afterwards pious hands strewed flowers on the spot from which the heroic soul went to heaven. "The memory of the just is blessed." Every one of the mob is long since forgotten, but the name of Savonarola still lives. He was one of the torches with which the hand of God kindled the light of the Reformation in the century following.

The view from the Michael Angelo's square, in the southeast of the city, is very beautiful. One sees the mansions nestling on the quiet hillsides around it. To the south is Michael Angelo's tower from which he looked upon the city which delighted to do him honor.

To the north and west is the city with its houses having gray walls and red-tiled roofs. The city does not look pretty. It looks old and gray, but the view is exceedingly picturesque. The mansions are strongly built. They were erected and first nhabited in troublous times, when it was necessary that every man's house be his castle. Remains of the old Roman wall are still to be seen. Taking it all in all, Florence is rich in art and history, beautiful for situation, and picturesque in appearance. We think of the grand old city with pleasure.

CHAPTER VIII.

Rome, Scenery on way to—The Corso—Peasants going to town—Population and Ruins—The Forum—Arch of Titus—Mamertine Prison—Paul in Rome—Capitoline Hill—Tarpeia—Nero's Palace and Gardens—Baths—Fountains—Colosseum — Anecdote — Pantheon — Catacombs — Churches — St. Angelo.

WE left Florence for Rome at 7:15 a. m. We made the distance of one hundred and sixty-two miles in five and one-half hours. For the first hundred miles of the journey the scenery is little different from what it is at Florence. The country is rolling. Old towns and old castles crown the summits of the hills. Some of these castles are as old as the religion of Christ.

It was a cold, rough morning, snow was seen on the hillsides—a sight rarely witnessed here—but the grass looked green. The olive trees were covered with minute white blossoms somewhat resembling our cherry blossoms. Shepherds watching their flocks, accompanied by large black dogs, could be seen on the hillsides. There are no fences. The landmarks are stones and trees and ditches. About seventy miles from Rome the train enters the wooded valley of the Tiber. The road runs along the gravel beds formed by the Tiber, which here is a mere creek. The small branches are cut from the trees and trimmed and arranged in large piles near the railroad; here they are loaded on cars and sent to Rome. Wood is scarce and dear in Italy. Everywhere the hotel keepers charge twenty cents for a mere armful, which is not sufficient to warm a room for more than an hour. As one comes nearer to the Eternal City, the soil becomes more fertile. Great herds of magnificent cattle are seen in the fields. The valley is broad, and not unlike our own valleys. One sees few vehicles on the roads. Ox-carts are frequent. Oxen are used in plowing. They seem to be real quick in their movements. As you approach the city, the ground becomes very marshy. The eucalyptus tree is planted in great rows to counteract the malarious influence of the marshes. The houses, which were not so numerous, are now more thickly built in the valley. Soon the dome of St. Peter's appears to the right of the swiftly-moving train. A few minutes more and the cars sweep through the old walls, and we are ere long at the railroad depot in the city, great in historic associations, great in religion, and great in crime.

Rome at present contains a population of about 300,000. Twelve years ago it was 285,000. In the time of Vespasian (A. D. 9–79) the city contained a population of nearly 2,000,000 people, of whom not less than half were slaves, which had been brought from every known country. Now there are no slaves in Rome, save the slaves of superstition. The ancient city was built upon seven hills. Three of these, the Aventine, Palatine and Cælian, are now desolate. Much of the old city lies beneath the new. In some places vineyards occupy the sites of ancient palaces. So much has the city changed that it is with difficulty that the ancient hills are traced. The Tiber still flows through the city, as turbid as in the days of Horace. New and beautiful bridges are being erected over this ancient stream. The channel is being cleaned, and Rome, the eternal city, seems to be awakening out of her sleep of superstition and indolence. The streets of the present city are narrow and circuitous. The principal street is the Corso. It is wide, well paved, and lined with the finest buildings in the city. The crowd here is simply enormous. It is the Broadway of Rome. The sidewalks of this street, as of all others in Rome, are narrow. The street is occupied by pedestrians who dodge about to keep from being run down. The peasants nearly all ride in carts. In carts drawn by a horse or donkey they bring their produce and their familes. These carts make a grotesque appearance when they contain three to six children together with the father and mother. They seem uncomfortably full. At every gate of the city there are several soldiers who, with long swords, examine the carts laden with produce as they come into town from the country. The Italian peasant must pay duty on many of his farm products. Taxes are heavy, and the condition of the peasantry is not an enviable one.

In this city of so many historical sites, such extensive ruins, such massive buildings, the traveler scarcely knows where to go first. We first visited the old city. Every reader of Latin classics knows the story of Romulus and Remus. Two wolves are still kept in an iron cage at the top of the steps leading to the Palatine, in commemoration of the legend that the two brothers were suckled by a wolf. From the Palatine the visitor looks down upon the great Forum. Here once sounded the eloquence of the most renowned orators of the Roman empire. It was in this Forum that the body of Julius Cæsar lay when Mark Antony pronounced his funeral oration. The Forum itself is twenty-five feet below the level of the present street. The site is covered with broken columns, the wrecks of its ancient glory. The Forum of Trajan, close to that of Augustus, was built at the beginning of the second century. This was the most magnificent Forum in Rome. Near by is Trajan's Column. This is a marble column 147 feet high and 11 feet in diameter at the base. A spiral band surrounds it, filled with illustrations carved in marble from Trajan's war. A statue of Trajan once surmounted it. Now St. Peter's figure stands there, as if watching the bones of the emperor beneath.

At the foot of the Palatine stands the arch of Titus, which was erected by him after he returned from his conquests in Palestine. The arch contains a representation in relief of captive Jews, and of what Titus found in the precincts of Herod's temple at Jerusalem. Though the arch is nearly twenty centuries old, the representations are distinct. From this arch we went to the street above, not far from which is a place of the deepest interest to all Christians. It is the Mamertine prison. Here Paul was confined in a damp cell for how long no one knows. There are two chambers, one beneath the other. A round hole in the middle of the floor leads to the lower chamber. It was in this chamber that Jugurtha the Numidian king perished of hunger and cold. From the chambers a subterranean pass leads into the Forum. Along this passage prisoners were taken to judgment. There is a spring in the upper cell which tradition says sprang from the rocks at the command of Peter. There is likewise an impression of the face of Peter on the wall, which was made by a Roman soldier thrusting the apostle's head against it. It is doubtful whether Peter ever was in Rome, so that these traditions are without support. That Paul was martyred in Rome every one admits. For the space of about two years Paul lived, wrote, and preached here. The Appii Forum and the Three Taverns, were the brethren met Paul as he went to Rome, are still known. Three Taverns is a place 33 miles southeast of Rome, and 10 miles from Appii Forum. On the *Via Lata* there is a small church which is said to occupy the site where Paul's "own hired house" stood, in which "he received all that came unto him." The pyramid *di Cais Cestio* near the gate *St. Paolo* is as it was in the days of the apostle. This was the last structure still remaining which Paul beheld on his way to execution beyond the walls. Not far from the city tradition points out the site where Paul was beheaded. The precise spot may not be known, but it was without the gate which now bears his name that Paul's great heroic soul went up to the Master to receive its well-merited reward. Though Nero lived in a golden palace, Paul was richer than he. Though the wicked tyrant had the power to condemn Paul to death, he thereby only liberated him from his bonds.

From the Forum it is not far to the Capitoline Hill. This hill was largely covered with public edifices when Rome was in the height of her ancient glory. The temple of Jupiter Capitolinus was somewhere on this hill. The exact site is not known. Here is the Tarpeian rock, named after Tarpeia, a Roman maiden, who commanded the citadel when the Sabines invaded the city. She opened the city on condition that the Sabines would give her what they wore on "their left arm," meaning their bracelets; but they wore their shields there too, so they threw those upon her as they passed in at the gate, and crushed her. She was buried at the Tarpeian rock. Afterwards those condemned to death were hurled from this rock.

The palace of the Cæsars on the Palatine Hill is one of the most extensive ruins in Rome. Each successive emperor raised new buildings, until the entire hill was covered. In the eastern part of this palace is the saloon of household gods. The broken statuary and the beautiful mosaic floors proclaim the magnificence and wealth of the place. The throne room is 117 feet by 157 feet. The reception rooms, the dining rooms, and many others, the use of which is not known, speak of the glory long since departed. Along the edge of the hill are the arched rooms in which the slaves had their quarters. The pictures in these rooms, together with the frescoes in the rooms of Nero's palace, are still fresh and pretty. The buildings, gardens and pleasure grounds of Nero after the great fire (A. D. 64) extended over three of Rome's seven hills. It was in these gardens that the tyrant burnt as torches innocent men and women. Vespasian destroyed the greater part of Nero's palace. Behind the palace of the emperors, in the valley *Via de Cerchi*, is the Circus Maximus, the place where races, games, etc., were held. It was a vast structure, which held 500,000 people. In the time of Julius Cæsar, it was not so large. It was destroyed by Nero's fire, and rebuilt by Trajan.

The baths of ancient Rome are interesting. The baths of Caracalla had accommodations for 2,300 bathers at once, whilst those of Diocletian could contain 3,000. The baths of Caracalla are beyond the city walls. One day a farmer was plowing when his plow struck a piece of marble which was attached to what seemed a huge block. This incident led to an excavation which revealed the Farnesian Bull. The work was continued until the baths of Caracalla were laid bare. This vast structure furnished steam baths, hot and cold baths. Besides the apartments for bathing there were public halls, libraries, porticoes for lounging, and places for athletic exercises. The floors are of the finest mosaics, which would make splendid relics if the guards did not watch so closely. In spite of them a Methodist D. D. succeeded in getting a pretty mosaic. I was no less fortunate. In this place the poet Shelley used to sit among the ruins and write poetry.

Rome has beautiful fountains which were an ornament to public places before the foundations of St. Peter's were laid. Whoever drinks of the waters of the Fontana di Trevi will come to Rome a second time. The Fontana Bernini is very old. The waters are brought from a great distance in pipes. Everybody who comes to Rome goes to see the Colosseum, the most impressive ruin in Europe if not in the world. It dates its origin with the first century of the Christian era. It is a vast structure, elliptical in shape, covering five acres of ground. It is nearly one-third of a mile in circumference. The outside of the walls is formed of huge square blocks of stone; they rise to the height of 156 feet. This vast structure was capable of seating 87,000 people; at the same time it afforded standing room for 15,000 more. The name Colosseum is derived from a colossal statue of Nero, which stood in front of it. The building was erected by captive Jews. It had no roof; the people found shelter beneath movable canvas. The dedicatory services lasted one hundred days, and five thousand beasts were slaughtered. The seats were raised in tiers. There are four rows. Each row has its own means of ingress and egress. It could be emptied of its vast multitudes in fifteen minutes. I stood where the emperor used to sit. Close to him sat the Vestal virgins. In this arena trained gladiators fought for the amusement of Rome's cruel and bloodthirsty inhabitants. Here pious men and women, youths and maidens, of whom heathen Rome was not worthy, offered their lives a willing sacrifice for the gospel of Christ. St. Ignatius was martyred here. There is one pleasing anecdote in the history of this ancient building. It is said that a jeweler sold a lady brass for gold. She accused him to the emperor, who decreed he should be torn in the amphitheatre. On the day appointed the jeweler stood pale and trembling before the multitude, awaiting the lion. Finally a trap-door beneath the sand of the arena lifted and a lamb came forth. The lady again complained, when the emperor said, "You were deceived, and so was he; be satisfied." Some of our company visited it by moonlight. The scene is impressive. One thinks of the many who here listened to the roaring of the wild beasts in the dens beneath the arena, knowing that they would soon feast upon their life-blood. God grant that no more in the history of the world such awful scenes may transpire as were witnessed here for ages.

The Pantheon is another monument of ancient Rome's greatness. This, as the name implies, was dedicated to all the gods. Its walls are twenty feet thick, and the portico is over one hundred feet wide and forty-two feet deep. Sixteen Corinthian columns of granite, four feet four inches in diameter and thirty-nine feet high, support the portico. The dome is a grand triumph of ancient architecture. The circumference of this dome is exactly the same as its height. It is open in the center; the opening served as a ventilator and for the transmission of light. In the wall are still to be seen the niches in which the images of heathen gods once stood. The inscription over the portico tells the visitor that this magnificent temple was built by Agrippa. It is therefore older than the Christian era. The earthquakes of nineteen centuries have failed to hurl it to the ground. Pope Boniface IV. consecrated it as a Christian church more than twelve centuries ago. The ashes of Raphael, and those of Victor Emanuel, sleep in this wonderful building.

Everybody has heard of the Catacombs. Most people think they were excavated by the early Christians. They are really the quarries from which the stone was taken for the construction of the magnificent buildings in Ancient Rome. It is asserted that some of them are older than the days of Romulus. It is said that every one of the seven hills is "perforated and honey-combed by passages, dark galleries, low corridors, and vaulted halls, where the sun never enters." Horace, in speaking of the caverns under the Esquiline hill, says: "This was the common sepulchre of the common plebeians." Christians and Pagans found tombs in these great caverns. That the Christians fled to these places for safety in times of persecution, is not as probable as some assert. These caverns were too well known to the enemy to be much of a refuge. That the same beautiful emblems and inscriptions are seen in the Catacombs that are so frequent on our own tombs, is certainly true. In traversing these damp, black galleries, and reading the inscriptions over the different tombs, one sees that the same sweet hope of a reunion in the better land cheered the soul of the Christian, that comforts us to-day as we stand at the open grave. The words "I am the resurrection and the life" were as blessed to the persecuted mourner then as they are to us to-day.

This brief description of Rome would be entirely too imperfect did we not say a few words with regard to the principal churches. In Rome the worshiper can hear mass every day of the year, and hear it in a different church every time. Of all the churches not one is dedicated to Christ; only one to the Holy Spirit; the Virgin has eighty-seven dedicated to her. Of all these churches St. Peter's is the largest, and in many respects the grandest. The first one of which I shall write is the church of "All the Angels." This church is famous because it contains the pictures which were at first in St. Peter's. Close to this church is a column erected in honor of the Virgin and her child. The church of Maria Maggiore is a fine structure; the place for this church was indicated by a miraculous fall of snow. The tradition is that here, and nowhere else, a snow had fallen; it was the place of which a pious monk had dreamed the night before as being covered by snow. When it was found that the dream was verified, the spot was selected. The tomb of Pope Pius the Ninth is in this church, and a part of the manger in which Christ was born. The church of St. John Lateran has porphyry columns brought from the Nile. In the baptistery of this church Constantine the Great was baptized. The church of *St. Pietro in vincoli* (Peter in chains) contains Michael Angelo's famous statue of Moses. The figure is in a sitting posture; the long beard comes to the waist; the eyes are piercing, the muscles are prominent, and the whole figure is so life-like that we are not at all surprised that the sculptor said to it: "Speak, Moses, speak." A crack in the right knee is said to have resulted from the stroke of Angelo's hammer as he uttered the words, "Speak, Moses, speak."

The church called "Sanctus Sanctorum" now contains the famous Pilate's Staircase. It consists of a flight of twenty-eight marble steps, now covered with boards, because they had been so worn by worshipers who ascended them on their knees. For every prayer said on these steps, the church grants ten years' absolution. These are the steps Luther was climbing when the words, "The just shall live by faith," rushed into his soul, and he arose at once. There are two marble figures at the foot of the stairs called respectively, "Betrayest thou the Son of God with a kiss," and, "The hour is come." There is also a picture of Christ, said to have been begun by St. Luke and finished by an angel.

In the monastery of the Capuchins and its church the chief place of interest is the room containing the bones of the deceased brethren. The order in this monastery had formerly but one grave. The last man that died was put into this, whilst the man who had died before him, if it was only a day, came out and was placed in position in the room containing the bones of all the deceased brethren. In this room I saw the bones of men arranged in every conceivable shape. Even the chandeliers, with all ornaments and pendants, are bones. It is a ghastly place. The custom is now prohibited by the government.

I was to the magnificent church of "St. Paul beyond the walls." This church was founded by Constantine in honor of Paula, a rich Roman lady. It was afterwards dedicated to the Apostle. The original church was burnt. The present is a recent edifice. On the outside are beautiful pictures in mosaics, the ground work of which is gold. Within all is magnificence. The medallions of the popes, and every pope has one, are not frescoes, but mosaics. The church abounds in alabaster, basalt, black and yellow marble, and porphyry. The ceilings are in white and gilt stucco, the floors are in polished marble. It has four rows of granite columns, eighty in all. The high altar is in the centre section of the arms of the cross, under a rich canopy. It is supported by four alabaster columns. Under this altar is the tomb in which it is said the ashes of the great Apostle repose. A chain said to have fettered the hands of Paul at his execution is shown here. It is in a cushioned box, and so highly venerated that the priest will not touch it with bare hands. This church is not finished, but it has already cost upwards of $25,000,000. It is used only on special occasions.

There is but one more of the churches of which we can speak. It is that one of which the poet has said :—

> "But thou, of temples old or altars new,
> Standest alone—with nothing like thee,
> What could be
> Of earthly structure in His honor piled
> Of sublimest aspect? Majesty,
> Power, glory, strength, and beauty, all are aisled
> In this eternal ark of worship."

St. Peter's, standing where it does, has forever consecrated the Circus of Nero, where so many Christians perished, and where St. Peter is said to have been crucified. Some one has said, "Take all the colossal beauty and strength and masterly proportions of the cathedrals in Europe, and combine them in one, and you have a conception of St. Peter's." Everything is so vast, so majestic, that it is only by degrees that the greatness of the work steals upon you. The façade, with its great pillars, supports 396 statues. These, together with the walls of the church, are blackened by age; but not so the inside of the vast edifice. The Cathedral is 613½ English feet long, the transept, from wall to wall, measures 446½ feet, the height of the nave is 152½ feet, the circumference of the pillars which support the dome, 253 feet; the height of the dome to the top of the cross, from the pavement below, is 448 feet. The steps leading up are broad, and easy enough to allow a loaded horse to ascend. To get an idea of the magnitude of the dome, we must go beneath and look up into the almost limitless space. As we look around, we see the immense size of everything. Two cherubs, apparently mere babes in size, hold a basin of holy water. We approach, and find that the limb is thicker than the trunk of a man. John the Revelator, in the ceiling, is writing with a pen (or quill) six feet long, but it seems scarce six inches. The paintings are all in mosaics. The altars, arches, columns, corridors, railings, and walls, glitter with gold. The high altar, underneath which St. Peter is said to be buried, is almost beyond description. Near the altar is a statue of the Saint in bronze, seated on a marble chair. Here is the toe which every loyal Roman Catholic kisses. It is worn away, not by the kisses, but by the constant wiping which everybody does before his kiss is impressed upon the great toe. There is a chair behind the pulpit of St. Peter, upon which is written,

"There is but one God, and Mahomet is his prophet." This chair is a trophy from the Orient.

St. Peter's is historical. Amid the Christmas festivities one thousand and eighty-nine years ago Charlemagne was crowned here by Pope Leo III. The place where the ceremony took place is still seen. One hundred and thirty-two popes are buried here. One could tarry here for weeks and listen to the worship which goes on night and day incessantly. St. Peter's cost $65,000,000. Every year nearly $41,000 are expended in its maintenance. There is quite a village of workmen's houses on the roof.

The Vatican is the pope's home. It is the most magnificent palace in Rome, if not in the world. The bishop of Rome in the fifth century had his house on this spot. We first went to the Sistine chapel, in which Michael Angelo achieved most of his deathless reputation. His work is now old and faded, but still glorious. The painting of the *Last Judgment* occupied him seven years. We visited the different rooms in the Vatican, and gazed like boys at a fair, in wonder and awe, upon its rich treasures of art. More than seventy thousand pieces of statuary have been taken from the ruins of temples and palaces in Rome. Very many have

ST. PETER'S BRIDGE AND CASTLE OF ST. ANGELO. Page 121

been gathered in this building. Here, too, are paintings from the celebrated artists of ancient and modern days. We went through the greater part of the pope's library; we also enjoyed a view of the gardens in which he walks. The largest piece of malachite ever found is in the Vatican. It was presented by the Czar of Russia. We were in the room where the young Prince Napoleon received the pope's benediction before he went to Africa, from whence he never returned. The pope's state carriage is a mediæval-looking affair, rich in gold. Notwithstanding all this wealth and glory,

"State for state with all attendant,
Who would change? Not I."

In passing back to the hotel, we go by the tower of St. Angelo, the citadel, the centre of which was the mausoleum of Hadrian. The castle is of little account as a fortress, and is used as a state prison. This was our last visit to any place of interest in Rome. Wherever we went to places of interest subsequently, and wherever we shall yet go, we cannot say to our souls,

"Omitte mirari beatæ
Fumum et opes strepitum que Romæ."*

---

* "Cease to admire the smoke, wealth, and noise of Rome."

CHAPTER IX.

NAPLES—Location—Relics of Antiquity—Churches—The People—Macaroni--Funeral—POMPEII—How to Get There—History—Pavement—Ruins and Population—Bodies Found—Progress in Arts—Café of Diomede—On Board "Ortigia"—Sicily—Buildings—Sailing on Mediterranean—In Africa.

NAPLES is the largest and most beautiful city in Italy. Here it is said the sun shines his brightest and flowers bloom loveliest. Naples, like most Italian cities, is very old. Its origin is lost in the mists of many years before the Christian era. It is generally supposed to have been a Greek city. The name is said to be Greek (Neapolis), signifying "new city," in contradistinction from Palæopolis, the older part of the city. Palæopolis is mentioned in history for having engaged in a war with Rome 330 B. C.

The city has a few relics of antiquity. Foremost among them are the temple of Castor and Pollux, the Julian Aqueduct, and the Catacombs, which are more extensive than those of Rome. The only entrance to them is through the church San Gennaro. They were used by the early Christians as places for worship and sepulture. St. Januarius (272-305), is buried here. A great many victims of the plague in the middle of the 17th century were heaped into these tombs. There are more than three hundred churches in Naples. The most interesting place, and the one most frequented by visitors, is the Museum. It contains a fine collection of curiosities and relics illustrating every department of life in Herculaneum and Pompeii. Far more interesting than all things ancient are the people of Naples themselves. They are the largest crowd of uncombed and unwashed, ragged and filthy people, I ever saw in Europe. The streets are filthy, and the sidewalks are narrow and crowded by men, women and children, buying and selling, sewing and gossiping, playing and quarreling. Along the road to the city we saw men working in stone quarries. They loosened great masses of rock, which their wives and daughters carried out of the quarries on their heads. One can see scores of women coming into the city to market with a good one-horse load on their heads. The better-to-do have donkeys hitched to carts or loaded with great baskets made of straw, filled with oranges, lemons, peppers; onions, cauliflower, etc. On top of these poor creatures, sprawled over the load, is a woman and child or a lazy man. Naples is the place where they make macaroni. The dish is quite popular, as every one knows, in America. I never did like it, now I abhor it. Along the street, especially along the road to Pompeii, one can see long yellow strings where dust and flies are thick. These have been prepared and put there by greasy, dirty-looking men, almost naked. In this country people have strong stomachs. It takes a good-sized cholera to upset them. There are some fine hotels, where the cooking is good, but I am speaking of the masses. With them a dish of beans and rancid bacon is a luxury. They have a dish called Pizza, made of dough, garlic, rotten cheese, and stale bacon. This they esteem a feast.

We took a drive along the hill overlooking the bay. We could see Vesuvius in the distance, whilst the city itself was at our feet. Above us the hillside was richly decorated by the most choice flowers, filling the air with their sweet perfume. I could not appreciate the meaning of the phrase, "See Naples and die,"* until I had taken this ride

---

* "See Naples and die," no doubt, originates in "See Naples" and a town below, the name of which is the Italian word for "die."

up the terraces overlooking the bay. In this ride we met a funeral. The hearse and coffin were literally covered with flowers. Pretty young girls, dressed in white, marched next to the hearse, singing a mournful tune, and bearing long tapers in their hands. They were followed by a long line of carriages. Everybody uncovers his head in Italy when he passes a funeral. Sometimes a band of music accompanies the funeral train. These people try to cover their poverty, and even the horrors of death and the grave itself, by an inborn joyousness.

Everybody who comes to Naples also goes to Pompeii. There are two ways to go to the excavated city—by the railroad, or by taking a coach in Naples. The traveler who wishes to save time goes by rail. The country through which the train passes is not pretty. The houses wear an air of poverty and neglect, which proves the inhabitants neither thrifty nor industrious. The dwelling-houses look more like forts than homes. They are mere stone walls, with roofs of tile, or stones and earth.

On arriving at Pompeii, the visitor pays a fee of forty cents; then he can go where he pleases, seeing the ruins, always followed by a guard, who sees that nothing valuable is taken.

Pompeii was destroyed by an eruption of Vesuvius on August 24, A. D. 79. For many years it lay buried, undiscovered and almost forgotten. In 1748 statues and other objects were exhumed in the digging of a well. Charles III. of Naples ordered extensive excavations seven years afterwards, and the amphitheater, capable of seating 10,000 spectators, was entirely uncovered. From that time excavation has slowly progressed, until now about half the city is uncovered. It had been a summer resort, with a population variously estimated at 2,000 to 20,000, and even fifty thousand. To this place the voluptuous Nero and other beastly Romans came for recreation and debauchery. There is full evidence among the ruins that they had abundant opportunity. By the earthquake the river Sarno was diverted from its course, and the sea, which washed the sands to the walls of the city, is now more than a mile from its excavated ruins.

Within the city walls, the first object which attracts attention is the stone pavement, consisting of square blocks of stone measuring about a foot. These stones have deep troughs worn into them by the chariot wheels of the ancient Romans. The stone is hard, but the streets are so narrow that the wheels always went in one place, hence the ruts. I do not know how the chariots passed each other; I suppose they went up some streets and down others, thus avoiding the difficulty of passing.

Some of the ruins are very extensive, proving that the population must have been more than 2000. The amphitheatre has already been mentioned. The theatre had accommodations for 5000 people. The temples of Fortune, of Isis, and of Neptune, were fine large places. The barracks of troops or gladiators were found located near the great theatre. Sixty-four skeletons were found here. It is supposed they were the guards who remained faithful unto death. Comparatively few skeletons are found, thus proving that the inhabitants had warning of their impending doom. In the museum, a small building near the gate, there is the form of a fat man with arms crossed. Here is a maiden with her clothing gathered under her arms, as if for flight from fire. A woman and child were found close together in death. The limbs of some are contorted, as if they had died in agony.

Pompeii, the exhumed city, gives the modern world a splendid idea of the domestic economy, the social life, and the arts and sciences of the ancient world. There is a house here which evidently was that of a wine merchant. There are earthen jars in it holding a barrel, whilst some hold no more than a quart. There are locks, beds, stoves, and cooking utensils, showing that the people possessed some of the conveniences and comforts of modern life. They had sliding doors, such as we have in our own parlors and larger apartments to-day. They had cut glass, and silver spoons of what we call the latest style, beautifully ornamented. The word "Welcome," cut in stone, adorned the door steps. Some of the floors are in beautiful mosaics of the finest marble. A room in the house of Diomede, evidently the bed-chamber of a maiden, has the representation of a dove picking jewels out of a casket. The whole is in mosaic of white and colored marbles. There was a fountain in the open court on which opened the various apartments. There are frescoes in an excellent state of preservation in red and yellow. The names of the proprietors of shops and residents of the homes of many have been discovered from seals and inscriptions found in the houses. Fine statuary and valuable jewels have been excavated. The houses are nearly all of stone, one story high. The upper stories, it is supposed, were of wood, and speedily consumed. But as these were used for storerooms and apartments for servants, little of value has perished.

After our walk, we went to a café for refreshments. This is in a lovely spot, surrounded by tropical plants, outside the walls of Pompeii. It bears the high sounding and historical name, "Diomede." Here we had a good lunch. When lunch was nearly finished, two musicians, with harp and violin, came in, and among other airs, played Yankee Doodle for us. Though the day was damp, we went back to Naples well pleased with our visit to Pompeii.

At 5:30 the same evening, we boarded the Italian steamer, "Ortigia" for Alexandria. The first part of our voyage on the Mediterranean was anything but pleasant.

Sicily is the largest island in the Mediterranean, being a little more than one-quarter as large as our State. At the northern end of the island is the whirlpool, caused by a current from the Black Sea, and called by the ancients "Charybdis." It was regarded a monster which twice every day gulped down the waters and twice cast them up again. Notwithstanding this wonderful proceeding, the waters are there to this day to make you seasick.

This island is the home of the mighty Ætna, which rises in solitary grandeur to the height of over ten thousand feet on the eastern coast. The climate is delightful. The thermometer scarcely ever rises above 92° Fahrenheit, nor falls below 36°. The day we were in the harbor at Messina was warm and wet. We bought delicious oranges, fresh from the trees.

Messina rises in the form of an amphitheatre from the waters of the strait. The houses are of dazzling white, whilst the dark mountains in the rear form a lovely background. It has some fine buildings, more than fifty churches, a large hospital, two theatres, a custom house, and other large buildings. It is defended by walls, citadels, and forts. Ships from every nation are to be seen in its beautiful harbor. After leaving Sicily, we had very pleasant weather. On Saturday morning (the third day out) we sighted the high hills of "Crete," under which the ship sailed in which Paul was being carried a prisoner, and in which he strongly advised the captain to winter.

It was now pleasantly warm. Our boat had a very light load, and rolled tremendously, even in a calm sea. In the evening, the moon arose in an unclouded sky, pouring forth a broad flood of silvery light across the sea, which looked like the path to the throne of heaven. On Sunday the wind blew in squalls, the ship rolled, and many of our company were sea-sick.

"Oh, E., think of our nice home," said a sea-sick lady to her husband. Then I thought of my nice home, too, and was home-sick. We could not have religious services that day. It was too rough to stand or sit still long enough to preach or listen. At luncheon, the captain said we would land at 4:30 P. M. Four hours afterwards we were afraid we could not land before Monday; but soon afterwards the light-house at the entrance to one of the finest harbors in the world was sighted, and at 6 P. M. we were in Alexandria. A happier company than we were I never saw, as we stepped on *terra firma*.

CHAPTER X.

Alexandria—Pharos—Pilot Boats—Crowd—Hotel "Abbat"—History of Alexandria—Pompey's Pillar—Libraries—Christianity—Drive—Houre of Antoniades—Square—Population—Merchants—Mohammedan women—Donkeys—Scenes on the way to Cairo.

AT the close of the last chapter we were too anxious to get ashore to say anything about the strange appearance of Africa along the Mediterranean. The coast seems lower than the sea, and has a grayish appearance. The first object which attracts attention is the light-house. It was at the entrance to this famous harbor, on an island seven stadia from the land, that Pharos, a light-house 550 feet high, once stood. It was one of the seven wonders of the world, having been erected as a monument for Ptolemy Philadelphus. The king ordered his name to be cut on the pediment, but Sostratus the architect first cut his own in the solid marble block, and placed over it in stucco that of the king. The stucco soon crumbled away, and the name of the architect for centuries greeted the eye of the beholder. This light could be seen for more than a hundred miles from the shore. Every vestige of the Pharos has long since disappeared.

As we approached the entrance to the harbor, we saw queer looking sail-boats. These were pilot-boats. In the hood drawn over their swarthy heads, they had rather the appearance of pirates, than friends to guide us among the rocks at the entrance to the truly magnificent harbor. These fellows were nude as to the lower portion of their bodies, but they were careful to have their heads well protected. The pilot did not come on deck to the wheel, but kept ahead of the ship with a flag in his hand, which he waved now to one side, and then to the other, thus indicating the course the vessel was to take.

I will never forget my first sight of the shrieking, jostling crowd of Arabs on the dock. To see them push each other and to hear their hoarse guttural cries was anything but inviting to us, the new arrivals. We had however nothing to fear; our company was expected and was met by the genial agent, who placed us in barouches, and just as night had fallen we were whirled past the custom house up one street, then out another, and we were at the hotel "Abbat." This hotel is built in true Oriental style. Palms and other tropical plants adorn the open court upon which the rooms of guests front. The reading room, smoking and coffee rooms, are simply recesses under the balconies on the one side of the court. Here we received our first Turkish coffee, very strong and black, in little cups holding a good large mouthful.

Before we go out sight-seeing I must tell you something of the history of Alexandria. For many centuries this city was the great centre of learning, wealth and power. Along these streets triumphant armies marched, and helpless captives were dragged, many centuries before the greatest modern nations had a name. Here the Ptolemies, Cleopatra, and the Cæsars reigned. Few land-marks of ancient Alexandria remain. There is a beautiful red granite column, called Pompey's Pillar, standing on the spot where in ancient times the worship of Osiris was conducted. This is the largest monolith in the world. It is one hundred feet high. It was erected by Publius in honor of Diodetian. The greater part of the ancient city lies buried in the sands, and with it are many of the famous relics of that once grand civilization. Of the obelisks that once stood here only one remains. One of them is in New York, another in London, and still another in Paris. Pieces of sphinxes and statuary are to be seen near Pompey's Pillar.

The people of ancient Alexandria were highly civilized. Books were written here sixteen centuries before Christ was born. The city had two libraries, the Serapeum and the Soter. The latter of these is said to have contained a copy of every known work. Had not Caliph Omar destroyed this valuable collection of 700,000 MSS. in A. D. 641, what light would it now shed upon many events and characters in history at which we can only guess! The destruction of this library was one of the most barbarous and unpardonable acts ever committed. The Christian Theodosius acted equally barbarously when he destroyed the vast treasures and exquisite statuary of the Serapeum. In this city Alexander the Great was buried in splendor, but not a vestige remains to identify the spot. In Alexandria the Hebrew Scriptures were translated into Greek B. C. 280. At that time Greek philosophy and culture were at their height in this city. There were Christian churches in this place when the Druids were still practicing their Pagan rites in England. Here Peter preached, and Mark suffered martyrdom. Origen was converted to Christianity here, after he had vainly endeavored to combat the doctrines of Christ with his philosophy. Other famous men in the early church, such as Athanasius and Cyril, were educated here. Apollos was born in this city.

Two hundred and fifty years after Christ was crucified, the whole of central and upper Egypt were Christianized. To this day there are some pious God-fearing men and women among the Copts, who know and study the New Testament. Such in brief was Alexandria before and for five centuries after Christ.

We took a drive through the principal streets of the city, and along the canal which brings the dirty water and the commerce of central Egypt from the Nile. On the banks of the canal we had the pleasure of visiting the mansion and grounds of Antoniades, a wealthy Greek. The servants wore a blue upper garment with white fringe, which gave them a neat appearance. The mansion itself is pretty, with its mosaic floors, its pictures and tapestries. The grounds are beautified by the tropical foliage and tasteful walks. When the winter winds howl in the Pennsylvania mountains I could reside in this mansion for a month or two, but not always would I live there.

The square of Mehemet Ali, with its fountains,

its statue of Mehemet Ali, its pretty trees and its large magnificent buildings, is the finest in Africa. One can scarcely realize, as he sees the splendid stores, fine-looking people, luxurious hotels, offices and equipages, that he is in Africa. There are some fine, well-paved, well-lighted and clean streets such as are not to be seen in the great metropolis Cairo; but then there are narrow, filthy and crooked, streets. Alexandria to-day is a great sea-port. The finest ships that sail on the Mediterranean come here. Like all sea-port towns, it has many haunts of vice. As soon as the shadows of night fall these are made brilliant with lights and hilarious with music. The city is rapidly becoming as populous as it was in ancient times. It to-day numbers no less than 200,000 people. There are to be seen on the streets men and women of every race and nationality under the sun. Here the traveler for the first time sees the turbaned Turk in his little bazaar, ever anxious to sell to you, and, if possible, to cheat you. These fellows always ask three times what they expect to get for an article. A dealer in precious stones had a real nice stone for sale. He asked twenty-five dollars for it, and was offered five dollars, which he at first laughingly refused, but after considerable bargaining he accepted it. A few mornings afterwards he saw the purchaser and began to weep, saying the stone belonged to a dear relative, and that he must have it back or receive five dollars additional. The purchaser then offered him the stone for half what he had paid, but the shrewd seller now went away without saying another word. When you make a bargain with a porter or donkey boy he is never satisfied when you pay him. He always wants something additional.

In this place you see the veiled Mohammedan women. As long as a girl is not engaged she goes without a veil. When she is engaged she wears a white veil. When married she wears a long black veil, which she never removes in the presence of a man except her husband. These fellows are so jealous that they will not allow their women, of whom they have as many as they can afford, to look at the moon unveiled, lest the man in the moon fall in love with them.

In this city the traveler first sees donkeys and donkey boys. For a franc (twenty cents) you can ride for an hour or two, as you wish; but the driver expects a *backsheesh* in addition. These donkey boys can trot behind a donkey, pounding the little animal and yelling for an hour, without the slightest inconvenience. They secure their animals from running away when not engaged by tying up one of the front legs. The traveler is not long in the Levant before he has great respect for the donkey. He seems to have more sense than any being about him. "I believe the poor creatures have souls," said a lady, "they seem so patient, so gentle." She afterwards changed her opinion, after she had been thrown in a mud-hole in Jerusalem. As a rule, however, donkeys are gentle, meek and very long-suffering! They have very queer names, such as Yankee Doodle, Telegraph, Mark Twain, George Washington, etc., etc.

After having seen all of Alexandria we cared to see, we started for Cairo. The cars on the road from Alexandria to Cairo are comfortable as any in Europe. The country through which we pass is level, and irrigated from the Nile by means of canals and ditches. The grass is several feet high, and the soil seems very fertile. The plain is covered with grazing sheep, musk oxen, cows and donkeys. Here and there we see the tents of Bedouins, pitched in groups, which give the otherwise peaceful country a weird appearance. The villages are mere mud-houses, one story high, with narrow alleys between them. Here and there is a little mosque about thirty feet high. It is white with a red stripe at the base of the dome. It is getting dark. We see shepherds leading their flocks homewards, and we think of the first verse in the Elegy :

> "The lowing herd winds slowly o'er the lea;
> The plowman homeward plods his weary way,
> And leaves the world to darkness and to me."

A few hours after dark we were in Cairo, the largest city of modern Egypt.

CAIRO.

CHAPTER XI.

Cairo—A donkey ride—Mosques—Slippers—Alabaster Mosque —Citadel—View—Mamelukes—"Well of Joseph"—University—Dancing Dervishes—Bazaars—Hotels—The street scenes—Backsheesh—Blindness and flies—Missions—The Copts.

CAIRO is the largest and most populous city in Africa, and is second only to Constantinople in the Turkish Empire. It lies on the right bank of the Nile, about a mile from the river, and has a population of nearly half a million of people. The city is seven miles in circumference. The houses of the poor are built of mud and sun-dried bricks, and are mostly only one story high. Those of the richer people are of wood, brick or Mokkatam stone from the hills not far distant. The streets are mostly narrow; all of them are illy paved, illy lighted, and illy watched. In case of a shower of rain, they become exceedingly muddy. I shall never forget a donkey ride I took after a heavy shower, through some of the principal streets of this truly Eastern city. I was covered with a black mud from head to foot, and looked very much like the poor fellows who sleep on the sidewalks in Cairo. In such a plight I had not been for many a day.

Everybody who comes to Cairo, goes to see some of the principal mosques. There are said to be 400 of these in the city; but only a few of them are of any note. We visited the mosque of El Hassan, an old but very commodious structure. The building looks very old from the outside, and almost worse within. The visitor takes his shoes off at the door and puts on miserable slippers, old and filthy from Arab feet. There is a large open court, in the centre of which is a fountain. In this the Arabs wash before worship. To wash is a part of their religion. If they do not pray often they do not wash often. The mosque of Mohammed Ali is the finest in the city. It is called "the alabaster mosque," because the inside of the building is lined with this beautiful stone. The courts of the mosque are paved with white marble and enclosed with beautiful columns. It has costly Turkish carpets on the floor, and hundreds of lamps suspended from above. The vaulted domes are overlooked by a clock-tower on the west. This tower is supported by four great piers, and "embraced by four half domes, with four smaller domes above the angles." From the ramparts of the citadel, the city of Cairo and the surrounding country are plainly brought to view. "The vastness of the city, as it lies stretched below, surprises every one. It looks a perfect wilderness of flat roofs, cupolas, minarets, and palm tops, with an open space here and there presenting the complete front of a mosque, and gay troops of dusky-skinned people, and moving camels." Immediately in front are the tombs of the Caliphs. In the court of the citadel the Mamelukes were slaughtered in 1811, by Mohammed Ali. This celebrated cavalry had an immense influence over the army and the country. Mohammed Ali suspected them of certain intrigues, and determined on their extermination. He accomplished this by alluring them into the citadel and then murdering them in cold blood. Only one, Emin Bey, escaped by riding his horse over the dizzy heights.

The "Well of Joseph" as it is called, supplies the citadel with water. It is supposed to be the work of the ancient Egyptians. It was discovered by Saladin. He found it filled with sand. It is two hundred and ninety feet deep, and fifteen feet in diameter. It is excavated out of the solid rock, with a spiral stair-case winding around like the thread of an auger to the very bottom. This stair-case is about ten feet wide, making the entire hole in the solid rock about twenty-five feet in diameter. "The water is raised by means of earthen jars fastened to an endless rope passing over a wheel, and kept continually revolving by mules or oxen stationed above and below." The jars come up full, discharge their contents at the top and descend empty. This well is worthy the skill and persevering labor of ancient Egypt, and is no doubt very old. Think of the size of the rock which can afford such an opening, so deep and so wide, without a break!

After leaving the citadel we went to the Mosque El Azhar and saw the so-called University, which is the largest Mohammedan school in the world. The building itself is very old, very dilapidated, and very dirty. The floors are covered by mats in three to five layers, and from all appearance must swarm with fleas. The dirty boys and men were squatted "Turkish fashion" around their teachers in different parts of the vast building. There are large chambers and courts in the building, and it may be that there are as high as fifteen thousand students in attendance, as is asserted by the officials. These "students" come from every part of the Mohammedan world. Their text-book is chiefly the Koran, which they transcribe on tin slates or tablets with stick and ink. There is apparently no order in the school, the students coming and going at pleasure. These fellows "earn their own living" as a rule whilst at the university. They "board themselves" by spreading a thin cake of rice or curry and flour on a flat stone, and waiting patiently until the sun dries it. Many beg for their board, and a scant fare it proves to be. Their "rooms" where they have their books, wardrobe, etc., are boxes consisting of apartments about a foot square. The whole affair is a burlesque on the name "university."

During my stay in Cairo I went to see the "Dancing Dervishes." These are a sort of monk among the Mohammedans. They live in a monastery which has a mosque attached to it. The buildings are dried mud and stone. The court and garden is a cool place, well kept. The monks wear long robes, and the faces of some of them are by no means bad-looking. They live chiefly upon what they can beg in the city, which, from the number of persons engaged in this business in Cairo, can not be very much. They also get fees from visitors, which are numerous. Their principal exhibition is given on Friday afternoon, the Mohammedan Sabbath. They assemble in the old mosque. There were fifteen or twenty of them squatted on the floor. Some were quite young, and one of them quite aged. There was an intelligent looking boy among them not more than fifteen years old. The man whom I shall call the master of ceremonies, began the performance by reading an extract from the Koran. The whole party now began to nod and grunt, first slowly, then more rapidly, until their heads became indistinct with the rapidity of the motion. Suddenly they] stopped, and immediately began to shake their heads from side to side. Thus they went through many motions, now and then varying the performance by singing a doleful air. They accompanied the motion of the body with grunts all through the "entertainment." Two of them played on a sort of a drum, which was accompanied by a clarionet in the hands of a third of their number. At length they arose and began a series of motions on their feet. One stepped out from among the rest and began a series of revolutions which made the beholder dizzy. He, strange to say, walked back at the end of his gyrations, as steady as when he began. The ceremony lasts for three or four hours, and is so silly and yet so wonderful that it must be seen to be appreciated.

Of course I visited the Turkish bazaars, which in Cairo are almost infinite in number and variety. Every trade has its own quarter. The manufactories of red slippers occupy several squares. The saddlers are also well represented. The jewelers and goldsmiths form an interesting group. Their wares are very pretty. The Turkish rugs, gold-laced jackets for men and women, are very artistic and very fine. The bazaars are in narrow streets into which the light of the sun can never enter. Some of these shops have goods worth thousands of dollars in little stalls in which an American grocer would hesitate to keep his horse. The stalls are old and filthy, and the "merchants" ask three times the price they expect to receive for their goods. The tradesmen are not all Turks and Egyptians: many of them are Jews. In these black, sombre-looking streets or lanes the weird music of the wandering minstrel, the plaintive wail of the beggar, the hoarse cry of the water carrier as he rattles his brazen drinking cups, are strangely interspersed. Besides these bazaars, Cairo has some fine stores on the wider and prettier streets. These are kept by Europeans.

The accommodations at the hotels, most of which are fine buildings, are very good. Our hotel had an open court, with a fountain in the centre. At one end were the stone stairs leading to the floors above. At one side of the steps was the office or "bureau" of information. On the other side was the large dining-room, the reading and smoking-rooms. The floors, the stairs, the walls, the roof, are stone. My room communicated with a stone balcony, overlooking a fine square. The "chambermaids" are not maids at all: they are Arabs dressed in white. The stone floors are covered with matting, not too clean. The beds are of iron, covered with nettings to protect the sleeping tourist from mosquitoes, etc. There is much of the etc., from which they cannot protect.

The streets of Cairo present a grotesque appearance, filled as they are with Mohammedan women, in their black veils and draperies, white veiled girls, half-naked boys with long-eared donkeys, turbaned Turks, swarthy Arabs, and easy going Caucasians from almost every country under the sun. The noise is deafening from the vehicles, the braying of donkeys, the hoarse shouts of Arabs as they try to gain your attention. The mothers march with stately strides whilst their infants are perched in silent majesty astride the mother's shoulder. Now and then the street scene is enlivened by the gay uniforms of a squad of British soldiers and their merry music. Frequently a gayly-dressed herald runs in advance of the coaches of the pasha and his attendants, so as to clear the way for the illustrious procession. Of course the water carrier is there, as among the bazaars. He cries *aqua buono!* (good water) but more frequently he shouts the Arabic word, *moya! moya!*

Here is a fellow with an immense bundle of sugar cane on his head, which he has brought to town to sell to the hungry street Arab, who lives upon this and a coarse cake. The fellow with the basket on his head mounted with a curious lamp, has the coarse cake or bread first mentioned, which he sells cheap enough. If it has been on his head long enough, the purchaser has a chance to get a little fresh meat with the bread. Many of the great throng of half-dressed, greasy and dirty people literally live on the street. At night they lie on the sidewalk in great rows, the head of one resting on the feet of his neighbor. They cover their heads; the rest of the body is not so important.

The condition of the poor people is pitiable in the extreme. The street scenes of Cairo are ludicrous, interesting, and at the same time sad. Men, women and children, sit along the road flat down in the dirt. They have corn, sugar cane, a little fuel, Arab cakes, or something worth very little, for sale. They no sooner see you than they cry for *backsheesh*. They are apparently as well satisfied if you give them nothing (that is what we usually gave them) as when you give them something. They never get enough.

There are a great many blind people in Egypt. One reason for this total and partial blindness is because the people think it a sin to chase the flies which sit in swarms on their faces. I have seen babies on the shoulders of their mothers literally covered with flies. The flies really eat the eyes out of the heads of the poor creatures. The ignorance, filth and superstition of these people is appalling.

The United Presbyterian Church has a prosperous mission in Cairo. It occupies a fine large building in the central part of the city. The building contains a chapel, a school-room, and living rooms for the missionaries and their families. An English service is held every Sabbath.

I attended prayer-meeting on Thursday evening of my stay in Cairo. We had an interesting meeting held in the parlor of the mission buildings. The audience was composed of Americans, English soldiers, and Arabs. There is quite a contrast between the children who attend the mission school and those who run on the street.

The Copts are the most interesting and most civilized people of Egypt. They do not speak the Arabic language; but they have a language which is said to approach, nearer than any other, the language of the Ancient Egyptians. It has greatly aided in interpreting the monumental inscriptions. The Copts are nominal Christians. They follow the Jacobites in believing that the human and divine natures in Christ constituted one nature, and one will. Their marriage ceremonies are lengthly and elaborate. The bride and groom are crowned, and the bride steps over the blood of a slain lamb at the door of her new home. The Coptic population numbers about 250,000. They are presided over by a patriarch, who resides in Cairo.

We made Cairo the centre from which we took various trips into the country, and villages around the city. These trips, and what we saw, will be described in the following chapter. Cairo itself contains, as everybody knows, no antiquities. The city was founded about A. D., 970, and is therefore not as old as many cities in Europe.

CHAPTER XII.

BOULAK MUSEUM—Arab Market—Old Statue—Raphsapha—Jewelry— Mummies of the Pharaohs—Value of these discoveries—Road to Great Pyramid—Arabs and recommendations —Sphinx—Size—Ascent of Cheops—Scenery—Dimensions —Chamber in the Pyramid—Who built Cheops?
MEMPHIS—Nilometer—Antiquity of Memphis—Arab village and Arab farming—Statues of Rameses II—Necropolis of Egypt—Mummies of "first born"—Oldest monument—Serapeum—Tomb of Tih—Frescoes—Way home.

IT was a bright spring-like morning in early March, when our party started for the Boulak Museum and the Pyramids of Gizeh. The geography of my boyhood contained a picture of the largest of these and the Sphinx. I always gazed on this picture with a sort of awe. This feeling was deepened when I caught my first glimpse of the pyramids, immediately after we left Cairo. I said to one of my companions in the barouche, "There are the pyramids!" "Oh," said he, "these are too close to Cairo to be the pyramids of Gizeh." I could only reply, "Wait and see."

In going to the pyramids the tourist crosses the Nile over a splendid iron bridge. There is a

(153)

market place immediately beyond the bridge. Here country people, donkeys, camels, flies and lice, sugar cane, oranges, candies, salads, sheep, grass, baskets with eggs, coops of palm-wood containing chickens, are indescribably mixed. Some are sitting on the ground around a dish out of which they take their morning meal. We are now well on our way, and soon the drivers enter the gates into extensive shady grounds, in which stand the buildings of the new but already famous *Boulak Museum*. Formerly this museum, or rather a very small part of it, was located in the city. Now it occupies the palace of Gizeh, about five miles from the heart of the city. It contains the most celebrated and extensive collection of Egyptian antiquities in the world. I can only mention a few things of the many I saw there.

The most interesting wood carving is a statue; the right arm hangs at the side, the left hand clasps a stick. The features and the style of clothing are perfect. It is estimated that this statue is from thirty to thirty-five centuries old. It was buried for centuries beneath the sands of the desert. It is a remarkable fact that the oldest tombs of Egypt contain wooden coffins and idols, in a high state of preservation. There is also an altar here of the purest alabaster. It was found on the right bank of the Nile, and is supposed to have existed in the days of Moses. There are numerous stone gods here. The statue of Raphsapha ("the man who follows Cheops") is interesting because it was found in the south-east corner of the Great Pyramid. This is a colossal statue which was finished before the foundations of Hebron were laid or Abraham pitched his tent beneath the oak of Mamre. There are figures here, playing the harp and flageolet, which are supposed to be thirty-six centuries old. These prove that these musical instruments were used very early.

One of the most interesting exhibits is the collection of jewelry which belonged to Queen Aahholep. She lived in the eighteenth dynasty, that is thirty centuries ago. Many of our "modern styles" of jewelry have evidently been copied from this, and equally ancient specimens. Not far from the collection of jewelry is the mummy-case of this woman. Her picture is on the outside of the case, and shows her to have been a woman of prepossessing appearance. I saw some carpenters' and masons' tools close by. The stone plummet is exactly like that of to-day.

The most interesting part of the collection is the group of mummies of the Pharaohs. "The Tombs of the Kings," so called, are situated among the cliffs, three miles west of Thebes. They contained no mummies when discovered, and it was for a long time a question what had become of them. A few years ago thirty-six mummies of the ancient Pharaohs and their families were discovered in a gallery two hundred feet long and thirty feet deep at the base of the Libyan Mountains. They had been brought here ages before, to protect them from the hands of vandalism. A number of these are now in the museum in the palace of Gizeh. These bodies are in a wonderful state of preservation. What is so strange, is that even the flowers which were left with the dead look as fresh as if they had been buried only a few weeks, instead of several thousand years. The cases in which the mummies were enclosed are richly decorated. One of them is overlaid in gold, and the name of one of these royal personages is set in precious stones.

I saw the mummy of Sethi I., whom Joseph is supposed to have served as Governor. I also saw the mummy of Thothmes X., the father of the man who erected the obelisk now in Central Park. I also saw the mummy of the man who erected the obelisk. The Pharaoh who ordered the destruction of the Hebrew boys is here. He is noted for the length of his arms and the murderous expression of his countenance. Near by him was found the beautifully embalmed body of a woman. This is no doubt the daughter who rescued Moses from a watery grave. With each body was found the heart of the individual, in a bronze urn or alabaster vase. We are thus permitted to gaze upon the very heart which God hardened so that its possessor would not let His "people go." If in all the realm of poetry or fiction there is anything more strange, I have not heard of it. The Rev. C. Cobern, Ph. D., truly says, modern scholars are "more accurately informed about the ancient history of Egypt than was the whole college of Heliopolis in Herodotus' time. To-day Ebur can paint a picture of Thebes in the days of Moses, with more accuracy and detail than Becker could of Rome, or Delitzsch of Jerusalem in the days of Augustus. The whole life of Ancient Egypt is open to us. We have the autographs of the contemporaries of Moses, and know the names of men who must have elbowed him on the street or bowed to him at court.* I began to realize as I

---

* In Homiletic Review for December, 1889.

left the museum, that I was now of a truth in Egypt.

> "Egypt! from whose all dateless tombs arose
> Forgotten Pharaohs from their long repose."

The road to the great pyramid from the museum leads in a direct line for a distance of about five miles, through a most fertile district. The road is shaded on either side by large acacia trees, thus rendering it the most pleasant carriage drive in Egypt. As we approached the pyramids, my friend at my side said, "Well S., I guess you were right; that is Cheops." And so it proved. When we were within three miles, we were sure it could not be more than a mile away. When we at last reached the hotel, within two hundred yards of the great pyramid, we were not sure but that it might still be miles away. The air is so clear and the pyramids so vast that distances are very deceptive. Half an hour before we got there, Arabs came running towards us with "antiques" for sale. They had little gods, images out of the mummy pits, coins, alabaster, and everything imaginable. In vain does the visitor tell them that he does not wish to buy. They can keep up a break-neck speed alongside of a barouche for

SPHINX AND PYRAMIDS.

hours, without apparent wearying. "Good antiques, very good," is their constant cry. "You no buy? Me sell cheap." One fellow insisted on being our guide. He had what he called "gud recommendazion." It read, "Do not trust this fellow; he is the biggest fraud and liar in the whole gang." This paper was duly signed by the name of a man from Chicago. We did not engage him.

After taking a luncheon in the Khedive's house, within a stone's throw of the great pyramid, we took a walk. We first went to the Sphinx. There is nothing but sand around this and the Pyramids which makes walking difficult. Some of our party thought they would try camels, but they were glad without an exception to dismount at the Sphinx and walk back. Everybody knows that the Sphinx "has the head of a man and the body of a lion," representing wisdom and strength. The head, neck and a part of the fore legs is all I saw. The shifting sands bury this colossal image as often as it is excavated. It was an idol in the days of Egypt's glory, as is attested by the sanctuary in front of the image, and the altar between its paws. A monumental tablet older than the pyramids has recently been discovered by M.

Mariette. It contains, in hieroglyphics, a list of all the Egyptian deities. Among them is the Sphinx, known as Hor-em-khoo "The sun his rest." This huge idol measures one hundred and forty feet, not including the fore paws, which extended about fifty feet in front. The head including the helmet is one hundred and two feet in circumference, and the body back of the neck forty feet in diameter. For a franc an Arab climbs up one of the fore-legs, walks over the mouth and sits on one ear. The drifting sands of the desert have disfigured this great idol, but the red paint that was put there centuries ago can still be seen. The whole gigantic figure is cut out of the solid limestone. When the Sphinx was cut out of eternal rock, and under whose direction the chisels which completed the mighty task were wielded, no one knows. Its origin is shrouded in mystery.

After our return from the Sphinx and his temple we were ready to ascend Cheops. Two apparently good-natured Arabs snatched me, and away we went. The steps or stones protruding from the sides are two, three and four feet thick. The Arabs scramble cat-like up these, and pull you after. They frequently asked whether I was tired. When I did rest they tried to sell me relics "from the doombs." In about fifteen minutes we were up. The scenery is sublime. On the one side the fertile valley of the Nile stretches like a great picture with its villages and the city of Cairo, with the Mokkatam hills in the distance. On the other side are the apparently interminable sands of the mighty desert. After singing "My country, 'tis of thee," we descended. I was preceded by my guides. I jumped from stone to stone, they holding my hands. The next three days I was so stiff I could scarcely ascend or descend the stairs in the hotel.

This pyramid is of vast dimensions. It is 764 feet square at the base, and rises at an angle of 52 degrees to the enormous height of 480 feet. It contains ninety million cubic feet of masonry, and covers an area of more than thirteen acres. The stones are nearly all very large. Some of them are twenty to thirty feet long and from three to five feet thick. From it the city of Cairo in Egypt could be built, or the city of Washington, in our own land, with all its public edifices.

All of the pyramids have chambers in them. The entrance to the Great Pyramid begins fifty feet above the base. The passage is three feet five inches wide, and three feet eleven high. The passage ascends at a moderate incline (twenty-seven degrees) a distance of a hundred feet, when it turns to the right, where the visitor is compelled to creep through a hole only fourteen inches in diameter; then the passage continues as before, to a gallery which leads to a chamber thirty-four feet long, seventeen wide, and nineteen high. The chamber is in red granite, beautifully polished, and is 350 feet from the outer entrance. There are two chambers. I have described the larger. This room was first entered, so far as we know, in A. D. 850. Nothing was found in it except the large, lidless sarcophagus which stands there to-day. Who built this mighty monument of antiquity will probably forever remain a mystery. Josephus believed that many of these pyramids were erected by the Hebrews, which is quite probable, inasmuch as some of them are built of sun-dried brick without straw.

It is believed by some archæologists that Joseph built the Great Pyramid with the labor of the people who were gathered in the city during the famine, and supported from the public store. It may have been erected as a depository for valuable records, and for astronomical purposes, as is asserted by many. The body of Joseph may have originally reposed in the now empty sarcophagus. His brethren, it will be remembered, promised to remove Joseph's body from its resting-place, and carry it with them to the land of promise. What a discovery that would be, if the embalmed body of Joseph would one day be found in a rock-hewn tomb in Palestine! The hieroglyphics on the Great Pyramid without doubt refer to Joseph. The cartouch found above the king's chamber containing the name Suphis (Joseph), is identical with the one in Wady Magharah, on the way which the Israelites journeyed to the land "flowing with milk and honey."

On the thirteenth of March, a number of us boarded a steamer on the historic Nile, for a trip to Memphis, the Noph of Scriptures. On the way to this historic city the traveler passes the Nilometer on the island of Rhoda. It is a well eighteen feet square, with a pillar in the centre, upon which the rise and fall is indicated by a scale divided into seventeen cubits. A cubit is about twenty-one and a half inches in length. The building surrounding the Nilometer stands in a beautiful garden. This building is covered on the dome and walls with passages from the Koran. It was erected in A. D. 848. It is probable that

Nilometers existed in the time of the Pharaohs. The people were taxed in proportion to the amount of water put on the land. These indicated the amount. Now they are useful in determining how far the canals for inundating are to be opened and how far to prepare for the overflow. The Nile at Cairo rises as high as twenty-five and twenty-six feet above low water. Egypt is the gift of the Nile. Were it not for the overflow of this wonderful river, Egypt would be one vast desert. Memphis is about twelve miles by steamer south of Cairo. It was founded by the first king of Egypt of whom history gives us any account. It was for a thousand years the capital of Egypt, and the finest and largest city in the land. Here Joseph had his home. Here he was falsely imprisoned, here he was vindicated, and here he rode in the first chariot of the land. Here Moses spent his boyhood, and here he wrought those stupendeous miracles which have continued the wonder of the ages, and the stumbling-block of infidelity.

No doubt some if not all of these pyramids which still stand the monuments of misguided ambition, were erected by the enslaved Hebrews. The embankments which once protected the city from the inundation of the Nile, have been washed away; the overflowings of the river have nearly obliterated the site of where was once such pomp and glory. There is an Arab village with its stone and mud houses, its narrow alleys, its mud walls, and the filth and squalor that is so characteristic of Arab towns. The place is surrounded by a beautiful grove of date-bearing palms. Here was the grand temple of Osiris. Broken columns, mounds of sun-dried bricks and huge blocks of granite, are all that remain of its ancient splendor. Here is a statue of Rameses II, the Pharaoh of the oppression. An outline of his daughter (his wife, some say) is hewn on the lower end of the back of the statue of the king. This statue was one of the two which stood in front of the gateway leading to the magnificent temple of Osiris. The face looks young, and the ladies of our party said he was "good looking." At the side of the monument is a cubical block recording a visit to King Hezekiah, in Jerusalem. A little further on we came to a second statue of the same king, representing him when he was forty years old. This statue, it is said, was originally sixty-five feet high. In front of the great temple was a large lake, many acres in extent. It was in this temple that they crowned the Egyptian kings, from Menes to the Ptolemies.

Back of these ruins, I obtained a good idea of Arabian farming. There are of course no fences. Canes placed upright along the path on which we rode, showed where the ground had been planted. Beyond these canes were long rows of onions. Between the rows of onions, cucumbers and salad were planted, ready at that time (March 13) for the table. The soil is very fertile, but the natives carry a fertilizer (black ground from the river) inland on the backs of camels.

Five miles from where we disembarked we struck the Libyan desert and the Necropolis of Memphis. For miles the country on the edge of the desert seems literally covered with ancient broken pottery, the remains of the old city. This cemetery in the desert is the oldest and largest burying place in the world. It extends from the Pyramids of Gizeh on the north, to those of Dashur on the south, a distance of more than a score of miles. It is estimated that it contains at least 25,000,000 human corpses. The Egyptians embalmed animals, such as birds, cats, etc. Millions of animals are contained in these vast fields of the dead. I saw skulls and the larger bones of bodies which had been placed here three thousand years ago. The Arabs use these remains for fertilizers. The linen (and it is the finest imaginable) in which the mummies were wrapped, is exported in vast cargoes to Europe, and even America, for the manufacture of paper. In some of the pits hewn out of the solid limestone, the bodies of the poorer classes are piled one upon another, like pieces of wood in layers, two and three feet deep. These are all as well preserved as the Pharaohs in the Museum, and were no doubt contemporaneous with them. These are the people who saw Joseph and his brethren in the days when Israel was honored in the land of the Pharaohs. It is supposed, from the fact of the great rows of mummies hastily embalmed, (all being young persons, not emaciated as if sick for a long time, but round and plump,) I say, that these are the first-born "from the Pharaoh that sat on his throne unto the first-born of the captive that was in the dungeon"* that perished in that awful night when Israel left Egypt.

The city of Memphis no doubt took its name from a pyramid here which is built in layers diminishing as they go up. If this is so, this pyramid is the oldest monument in the world! There are eleven of these pyramids, but this is

*Exodus xii. 29.

evidently the oldest. These are known as the Pyramids of Sakkara.

North of this pyramid is the *Serapeum* or tombs of the sacred bulls. These are the bulls that were worshiped here. They killed these bulls if they did not die before they were twenty-five years old. Then they were dumped into a great well. If they died before being twenty-five, they were buried amid bacchanalian festivities in the Serapeum. When the calf for the making of another god was found, he was kept forty days at Nilopolis, then taken by water to Memphis, where he was attended forty days by naked women: then he became a god!

From this bull-worship the Hebrews obtained the idea of the golden calf which was erected in the wilderness when Moses was on the mount. Apis, or the bull, was regarded as the incarnation of Osiris, the god of the Nile. The vast tomb is hewn out of the solid rock. Over this tomb the temple of Serapis stood, "where the sacred cubit and other symbols were kept," and funeral services were held. After lighting tapers we descended into the vaults. In the vaults are granite sarcophagi thirteen feet long, eight feet wide and eleven high. Here the embalmed bulls were put.

The granite is polished beautifully. Ten of these monster stone boxes never had anything in them. These sarcophagi weigh sixty tons. They were brought here from immense distances.

We also visited the the tomb of Tih, not far from the Serapeum. This tomb dates back to the fifth dynasty, and is more than four thousand years old, yet the walls are as straight and perfect as if finished last year. The covering, and other parts of the passage leading to the tomb, have disappeared; but the rest is in an excellent state of preservation. There are three chambers, one leading into the other. These are all filled with frescoes and sculpture in bas-relief. The fourth is the sepulchral chamber. The frescoes represent scenes in his life. This Tih was a priest in Memphis, and very rich. There are harvest scenes, fishing scenes, and men bringing tithes to Tih, who receives them. In short, the principal acts of the man's life are here delineated. These frescoes lay buried in the sands of the desert for twenty centuries, unknown and unnoted, and yet they rival in perfection of colors the paintings of a Rubens or an Angelo. It seems as if a temple had been built over this tomb and divine honors were paid to Tih. There was a tube from above through which his devotees could speak to him in the tomb below. On our way back we passed through a Bedouin camp, and what was more remarkable, a shower of rain. Our backs were well soaked, but they soon dried again in the hot sun. We had scarcely gotten on board our boat before it rained very heavily. After luncheon we sailed back to Cairo, well pleased with what we had seen and learned at Memphis, the Noph of Scripture.

CHAPTER XIII.

Heliopolis—Temple—Phoenix—School of Philosophy—Obelisk—Spring—"Virgin's Tree" Garden of Cleopatra—Thebes—Temple of Karnak—Of Luxor—Hall of Columns—Addenda by Dr. Kirk—Ride up the Nile—The Nile—Asyoot—Blindness and Flies—Water lifts—Abydos—Columns—Luxor—Thebes—Karnak—Avenue of Sphinxes—Halls—Nautch dance—Tombs of the Pharoahs—View—Traveling on Nile—Ismailia—Ride through the Desert—Suez Canal—Port Said—Reflections.

ONE beautiful afternoon in the middle of March about a dozen of us drove to the site of Heliopolis, called in old Egyptian On and Ha-Ra. This was one of the oldest cities in Egypt. It was situated at the head of the Nile Delta, about eight miles north of Cairo. This city was famous for its temple of the sun and its learned priests. This temple was approached through an avenue of marble sphinxes and obelisks. The temple itself stood at one end of an inclosure three miles in circumference. The ruins of these walls can still be traced. Here the Phœnix was consumed. This was a bird of beautiful plumage, about the size of an eagle. It always lived five hundred years. At the end of that time it would come to Heliopolis and cast itself into a fire perfumed with spices. This fire a priest in the temple of the sun prepared on an altar for the bird's special benefit. The ashes remained on the altar for two days, when a worm would appear, then on the third day the revivified bird would arise and soar away more beautiful than ever.

The priests of this temple were skilled in all the mysteries and the philosophy of Egypt. Here in this celebrated city Plato studied philosophy and astronomy four hundred years before Christ was born. Moses received his training here, and in this city Joseph found a wife among the daughters of the high priest. We have many reasons to suppose that the ancient college at Heliopolis far excelled anything of that name now to be found in Egypt—the famous university, that burlesque on modern institutions of learning, not excepted.

There are few ruins at Heliopolis to-day, to tell its ancient grandeur. An Arab by the name of Abdallatif, living in the twelfth century, speaks of colossal figures in stone, standing and sitting, and some of them more than thirty cubits high. There is one lone obelisk standing here, a single conspicuous monument of the city's departed greatness.

This obelisk is nearly 5000 years old. It bears the name of Osortasen I, who lived 3000 years before Christ. Two obelisks were removed by the Greeks from this place to Alexandria. One of these is now in New York, and the other in London. The obelisk in the Place de la Concorde, is also from Heliopolis. It was near this monument that Kleber thrashed the Turks, on the twentieth of March, in the first year of this century. If this lone shaft of granite could remember and speak, what startling facts and momentous events it could rehearse ! It used to stand on an eminence, now the land is low all about it. I was compelled to walk through a pool of water to gain its side. The Nile has drifted millions of tons of soil into the low land. Beneath that soil, I doubt not, lie buried some rich treasures of ancient art and wealth. This place, at present, is famous for the only spring in Egypt. Near the valley of Matareah is a beautiful garden, from which we bought very cheap the most delicious oranges I tasted in Egypt. Here is the "Virgin's Tree," an old sycamore, underneath whose spreading branches the Holy Family are said to have rested, when they fled from Herod. The Arabs and Copts seem to venerate this tree, but when or how this tradition originated, I cannot tell.

Near this city was the magnificent garden of that talented and wicked woman, Cleopatra. Here she grew the Balm of Gilead, which she had brought from Judea. The soil is still fertile, and the country is beautiful. When the red sun sank to his burning bed amidst the sands, I could hardly realize that I was in the land of Goshen, nearly six thousand miles from home.

I have not, as the intelligent reader will know, exhausted the whole vast list of famous remains that have been found along the Nile, upon which was cradled the most ancient recorded civilization. The ruins of Karnak and Luxor, which once formed a part of "hundred-gated Thebes," are as interesting as any in Egypt. I can only mention these in this little volume. Thebes is a very ancient city in Upper Egypt. Our earliest reliable history does, however, not date further back than B. C. 1500. A large part of the city was built on an island in the Nile. About all that remains east of the Nile are the famous ruins at Karnak and Luxor, two modern villages near these famous ruins. The temple of Karnak which was dedicated to Jupiter Amnon, was connected by a magnificent avenue of statues and sphinxes with the temple at Luxor. A perfect forest of columns, no two of which are alike in sculpture or coloring, adorn these grand temples. The temple area was a square of ninety acres, one-third of which was covered by the building. Four gates, one to each cardinal point, led to the temple. Behind each gate were two others, separated from each other by proper intervals. These intervals or avenues were adorned with sphinxes. These gateways are the grandest ruins in Egypt. The "Hall of Columns," at Karnak is 329 feet long and 170 wide, and eighty feet in the clear. The stone ceiling rests on stone girders, and is supported by 134 columns, the highest sixty-six feet, and the lowest forty-two feet in length. Here, too, are obelisks and statues, all of which conspire to make this the grandest temple in Egypt, if not in the world. The temple at Luxor is second only to that at Karnak. It dates back to the time of Queen Hatasan, the supposed Pharaoh's daughter who adopted Moses, "She built this temple" is the record on the square. The coloring after the lapse of so many centuries in this temple is truly wonderful.

The time for us to leave the land of the Pharaohs came all too soon. We took our last look on the Nile, of which Leigh Hunt says:

'It flows through old hush'd Egypt and its sands,
Like some grave mighty thought threading a dream."

"After a five o'clock dinner, on March 12, 1890, we took carriages for the Ghizeh railroad station, a distance of about three miles from our hotel, the Hotel du Nil, and under the shadow, it almost seemed, of the Pyramids.* The first 230 miles, to Asyoot, was to be made by rail, at night, as we were to return the same way by daylight; the railroad being always in sight of the Nile. In the absence of Pullman sleepers, we were compelled to ensconce ourselves, for a night's rest, as comfortably as possible under the circumstances. Six of us occupied a compartment, with two double seats, facing each other, each the width of the car, and with genuine Yankee ingenuity we began to devise plans whereby we might best utilize the sleeping facilities of our compartment. This resulted in two occupying each double seat, foot to foot, and the other two taking the floor between the seats, the whole operation completed by a systematic dovetailing scheme. Thus we passed the night. We may have slept, but we cannot declare truthfully

---

*I am indebted to Dr. Harvey M. Kirk, of Columbus, Ohio, for the following account of a trip up the Nile.

that it was delightful repose. The atmosphere, as is usual at night in Egypt, was very chilly, and it was all we could do, with our shawls, or overcoats, wrapped about us, to keep warm.

"At about five o'clock the next morning, and just as daylight was breaking, our train suddenly stopped, and we were apprised that we had arrived at Asyoot, the Capital of Upper Egypt. Hastily gathering our effects together, we left the train, and after breakfast we were off on donkeys for Asyoot.

"The Nile, the 'river of life' of Egypt, has always been a mysterious river—mysterious as to source, annual inundation, and as to flowing the distance of 1,350 miles to the sea, without a tributary. It is referred to several times in Holy Writ. On its bosom, near Cairo, floated the infant Moses; not far distant, on its banks, the Holy Family took refuge in a cave to escape the wrath of an unjust ruler; its waters were turned to blood when the heart of Pharaoh was hardened.

"By the annual inundation, a thin layer of fertilizing mud is spread over the land, and the canals are filled with the precious water. Seeds and grain, spread broadcast, produce a bountiful harvest. The inundation begins in the latter part of June, reaching its highest point during the latter part of September; it remains at this point about fifteen days, when it gradually recedes. The best average rise is 24 feet above low-water mark. Should the water rise no higher than 18 feet, a famine would ensue. Should it rise 30 feet, a flood would be the result.

"Our path led us westward through fertile fields of the valley, to the City of Asyoot, a town of 25,000 inhabitants—at present the seat of a large market, and formerly the principal slave market, but abolished some time since. On the road, we passed by a school, under the auspices of the Presbyterian American Mission, containing nearly 200 students. Approaching the city, fifteen minarets and turrets can be counted. We passed directly through the city, then crossed a bridge spanning a canal, soon arriving at the base of a sandy mountain, about 400 feet in height. Cut in the face of the mountain, we see large holes, and are informed that they were formerly used as sepulchres. Dismounting, we begin the ascent. About two-thirds of the way up, we arrive at a very large cavern. This was used as a royal tomb 4000 years ago.*

---

*This is the place where, in 1878, an Arab discovered the tomb of the Pharaohs. He kept the secret for three years, but was found out through the relics which he sold.—S.

Passing into a corridor, we are led into a large hall, containing a number of smaller chambers or recesses. Continuing our ascent, our perspiring crowd ere long arrived at the summit, where a scene of rare beauty met our gaze. At our feet, as it were, and to the right, lay the Coptic city of Asyoot, with its tall minarets and rounded domes; to the left a little, the necropolis, white like alabaster. Beyond, the valley of the Nile, with its glistening, serpentine river near the centre, trimmed with living green, the whole flanked by the chain of Arabian and Libyan hills. Resting, and pondering the scene for a time, we return to our donkeys.

"Passing along the narrow streets, from 6 to 12 feet wide, lined on either side, some of them with bazaars with cross-legged, lazy-appearing, turbaned proprietors, stared at by the dirty half-clad populace, does not require any stretch of imagination to make one feel that he is indeed in the very heart of the Orient. The houses here, as well as all through the Nile villages, are constructed of adobe, or sun-dried mud, in the shape of bricks; serving their purpose very well in this hot climate where rain seldom falls; were it to rain hard, they would be melted, and their huts thus destroyed. The houses are of one story, sometimes with a flat roof covered with matting, sometimes having the same adobe roof, though dome-shaped. The floor is the ground, undecorated and uncovered. Dirt and filth predominate. Blindness, and partial blindness, exist to an alarming exent, caused mainly by the unmolested multitudes of flies which are allowed to gather around and in the eyes of the children, being never brushed away by the mothers or persons in charge; congregating so thickly about the child's eyes as to render the eyes invisible to an observer. This, together with the concomitant filth, is the most prolific source of blindness.

"Two familiar and oft-appearing sights are the palm groves and water-lifts. The former are very beautiful, with their huge, tall single trunks, and the large tuft of foliage at the top. The latter are constantly in sight, and are necessary adjuncts to the Fellaheen's success.

"The most common method employed to raise the water from the river to the irrigating canals on the shore, is by means of a skin bucket attached to a long pole, with a lump of mud on the other end to balance the bucket when filled with water, the whole resting upon a sort of frame. The bucket is operated by a man, who dips the bucket into the river and raises it by a hand-over-hand motion, and pours it into the canal on the shore. It often happens, when the bank is high, that two, three, or even four, of these 'shadoofs' are necessary to raise the water to the shore and turn it into the canal, through which it flows into smaller and more distant canals. We pass high hills on both sides of the stream, in whose sides are holes, or caves, used in days past as tombs. We also see lots of sheep, but they have inverted our rule here. Instead of having ordinary white sheep, with an occasional black one, they have all black sheep, with an occasional white one.

"We have plenty to eat; our cuisine is all one could wish in this part of the world, and a great deal better than we had expected to encounter We have breakfast at 8:30 a. m., luncheon at 12:30 p. m., tea and crackers at 4 p. m. on the promenade deck (over which is stretched a canopy during the hot part of the day), dinner at 6:30 p. m., and tea and crackers again at 8:30 p. m. We are now, 6 p. m., at anchor at a small village, and the perfume of orange blossoms is delightful.

"On the morning of March 15th, at about 9 a. m., we arrived at the village of Bellianeh. We took donkeys for the Temple of Abydos, six miles westward. We arrived in about one and one-half hours, and at the far end of a miserable mud village came all at once upon the ruins of the great temples of Abydos—piles of mammoth remains. Surrounded at once by a motley crowd of natives, all voracious for 'baksheesh,' from the old grey-headed priest of the household to the smallest of the tribe, the latter holding out its hand and lisping 'baksheesh,' simply because it was undoubtedly its first lesson in a, b, c. The first temple we see, the Temple of Sethi I., was built by order of Sethi I. about 1300 or 1400 B. C. This place is remarkable as being the birthplace of Menes, founder of the Egyptian monarchy, and here is also the place where Osiris was born, educated and buried. This has been a gorgeous temple, replete with wonderful sculptures and highly-finished hieroglyphics. The temple has two large courts, one containing twenty-four, and one thirty-six huge columns. A hall leading to the King's Chamber gives the names and cartouches of the 76 kings, from Menes to Sethi I., on a finely-executed tablet, called the New Tablet of Abydos. This tablet is one of the most valuable records ever discovered in Egypt, being a kind of key to the whole of Egyptian history.

"A little farther north is another ruin, the Temple of Rameses II., son of Sethi I. Not so much remains of this temple as of the former. Built by Rameses II. while on the throne, it is believed to have surpassed the former in grandeur. We see immense blocks of stone, granite, and alabaster, some of them twelve to fifteen feet long, and from four to five feet square at the ends. The roofs of these buildings were made by laying crosswise on their faces, from one architrave to another, huge stones, then arched and adorned with sculptures and hieroglyphics.

"At five p. m., March 16th, we arrived at Luxor, 450 miles above Cairo. Disembarking for a short ramble, we wandered among the ruins of the Temple of Luxor, which is just a short distance from where our boats anchor. Luxor is a moderate sized town, with the same attributes precisely as the other Nile towns. The town is built about the Temple. The natives are such infernal pests here, that one can hardly contain himself. They are continually dogging our steps, either begging, trying to sell us some worthless article, or endeavoring to tell us something in their pigeon-English. Thus it has been ever since we struck Africa, and the farther we penetrate the worse it gets. They follow us like a hungry horde, and it takes several native dragomen to keep them off.

"At this temple is the celebrated large obelisk, the companion of which occupies the site of the Place de la Concorde, Paris. Of course, it is understood that these obelisks always were erected in pairs. This one consists of one solid piece of fine polished red granite, 84 feet high, and erected where it is now standing over 3300 years ago. Here are several immense granite statues of Rameses II. no less than 25 feet high. The outer walls of the temple are ponderous affairs, built on the battery wall plan, thicker at the bottom than at the top, this one being about 25 feet thick at the base.

"After breakfast next morning we were rowed across to the west bank of the river, where we took donkeys for the temples of Thebes, about three miles distant. We first visited the Temple of Rameses II, also called the Ramesium. This temple was constructed about 2000 years B. C. The ancient city of Thebes occupied both sides of the river at this point, the west side being principally occupied by temples and palaces, and was also used as a necropolis. Here at the Ramesium is the giant statue of Rameses II, constructed from one solid piece of red granite. It is prostrate and broken now, but in its glory it stood over 50 feet high and weighed nearly 1,000 tons—the largest ever constructed.

"The Egyptians take no care of their monuments and ruins at Thebes—very much unlike the Italians, whose government realizes a considerable revenue from its ruins, which are strictly guarded by Roman and Italian soldiery. Other Theban monuments are the Tembles of Koorneh, Dahr-el-Bahree, Medinet Haboo and others, including the Tombs of the Kings. Other wonderful monuments are the two Colossi, which once stood before a temple, now standing alone in a vast plain like two giant sentinels. They are in a seated posture, and are sixty feet in height.

"At some distance, in a northerly direction, is the wonderful Temple of Medinet Haboo, erected by Rameses III. The ruins are apparently more extensive than the others, and date back nearly 4000 years. They were restored before the time of Christ, by Emperors Neva and Alex. Severus.

"Returning to our boats, tired and warm, we take our lunch, preparatory to visiting the renowned Karnak in the afternoon. After lunch, the next thing for each one was to get his *sine qua non*—the donkey. Starting northward, passing through Luxor, for about two miles beyond we rode through a fertile plain. We first pass under a mammoth archway, probably eighty or ninety feet in height, leading us into the famous Avenue of Sphinxes. This must have been a wonderful sight, ere time and vandalism laid their destructive hands upon these mighty works. There used to be two hundred giant sphinxes arranged on either side of the road. The pedestals still remain, the heads in most cases being broken off. This was one of the approaches to the great Temple of Karnak, there being seven equally as grand, of different designs, but having wonderful propylæ, arches and walks. The main feature, to the tourist, is the Grand Hall. Entering by an immense propylon, 370 feet in breadth, with a tower 140 feet high, we come upon a striking sight. This hall is about 170x329 feet. It contains 134 enormous columns, some of them, the middle rows, being 66 feet in height, without the capitals, and 36 feet in circumference, all carved and sculptured in a wonderful degree. Leaving this hall, as far almost as one can see there stretches out one immense pile of interminable ruins. Here is the largest and finest obelisk known, being 92 feet in height and 8 feet square at the base. It is said that in the palmiest days of Thebes and Karnak this obelisk was surmounted by a pyramid of pure gold. Erected nearly 1500 years B. C., this obelisk still stands as straight and perfect as though it were erected but yesterday, a striking example of the permanency of earthly things. Beside it is a smaller obelisk in almost perfect preservation. Another part of the temple, called the ruined sanctuary, is estimated to have been built over 3000 years B. C.

"'The whole structure dates back to the times of Sethi I. and the Rameses, from 1300 to 1500 B. C. The walls of the outside are 80 feet high, and 25 feet thick at the base, and the whole structure about one and three-quarters miles around. Wandering over this ruined temple, climbing over immense piles of ruins and debris, walking for hours, it may be, through various halls and chambers, one can only faintly realize the wondrous grandeur and pomp that once existed there. The various scenes pass before one's vision like a panorama, till finally, almost bewildered, one sits down to rest, and to ponder, and to decide for a certainty, if possible, whether what he sees is actually a reality, or merely a fleeting vagary of dreamland.

"After several hours we returned to our boats, following a different route from the one we came, the whole distance nearly, right alongside the river. We were thoroughly tired, but more than repaid, for the exertion of the trip to Karnak.

"This evening, by the payment of a small admission fee, we were entertained at the rooms of the American Consul by a Nautch dance, by three female dancers. They were dressed in white, with long pendant ear-drops. Their dancing consisted mainly in violent contortions of the body, accompanied by a gliding across the floor. During the ceremony two or three musicians dealt out harmony (?) from a fiddle and a kind of drum. One of the dancers did a very clever piece of balancing a lighted candle on her head while going through her manœuvres, even lying flat on the floor, then standing erect, without disturbing the candle. At the conclusion of the dancing, the servants brought in a genuine mummy, several thousands of years old, they said, which they proceeded to open, to our intense delight. The mummy proved to be that of a lady of rank, as she wore an anklet and a ring on her finger. Certainly it was a rare sight for Americans.

"March 18.—We rose at 4 A. M., breakfasted soon after, and before daylight crossed the Nile in boats to Thebes, thence to the Tombs of the Kings.

After a two-mile ride we stop for a while at the Temple of Koorneh, dedicated to Rameses I. by his son Sethi I., and in turn completed by his son, Rameses II., the Sesostris of the Greeks, about 1400 B. C.

"Remounting our donkeys, we make a long ride through bleak, stony places and narrow passes. We finally arrive at Tomb No. 2, the tomb of Rameses IV., constructed 1250 B. C. These royal sepulchres are situated in the valley of Bab-el-Molook. The tombs are excavated into the solid rock of the mountain, bearing resemblance to a large corridor or hall, gradually descending; several hundred feet in length, the walls highly decorated, with occasionally small anti-chambers in the sides, while the royal sarcophagus occupies the extreme internal end of this elongated tomb. After the burial the entrances to these tombs were covered up, so as to afford no trace of the spot. Already about twenty-five have been discovered. We visited also the tombs of Rameses III., VII., IX., and Sethi I. At 10 A. M., we lunched in front of Tomb No. 19, where we were all photographed in the act by our party photographer; after which we began the ascent of the mountain on foot, followed by our donkeys and donkey boys. Finally, tired and perspiring, we reached the summit, where we came, after a while, to a small plateau facing the Nile Valley, where we gained a splendid view of the Nile, the Valley, Thebes, Luxor, and Karnak beyond the river. Descending to the opposite side of the Libyan mountain, we come upon and enter the Temple of Dahr-el-Bahree. This is a peculiarly arranged temple, being built up against the mountain side, the mountain thus forming one side of the structure, and the courts being at different elevations up the mountain side. It was right in this immediate vicinity that the mummy of Rameses II. was found, now in the Museum at Cairo.

"Traveling at this season is still pleasant. Though the days are hot, the evenings and nights are delightfully cool. During the day time the sun's rays beat down with a tremendous force, even at this time of the year, and when in sandy places, the sand reflects the heat, thus aggravating the case.

"March 19.—We arrived to-day at Denderah, where we stopped off to visit the Temple of Denderah. We of course passed by here on our upward trip, but the conductor preferred us to see this place on the return trip. The Temple of

Denderah is on the west bank of the river, nearly opposite Keneh, on the east bank, and about 395 miles above Cairo. We take our donkeys again, and ride about three miles ere we arrive at the monument. It was built about 2000 years ago, consequently rather modern in comparison with the ancient structures we have been used to seeing the past two days. It is in a splendid state of preservation, with its massive columns and its heavy, receding or battery walls. The building is nearly perfect, roof and everything. The battery style of walls is coming into use again by our architects and builders in very heavy buildings, illustrating the proverb, 'There is nothing new under the sun.' The lower part of the building was dedicated to the goddess Isis, the upper part, the astronomical portion, to Osiris. Upon entering the building we first come into the grand hall, with its 24 great columns. There are several smaller rooms, or sanctuaries, with no windows, where it is supposed that certain rites were observed by the priests, in secret, and the Fates consulted; here are also crypts for treasures and sacred emblems. Into one room the king alone could enter.

"There is an interesting fact connected with the erection of this temple. Treated as slaves by the

Greeks, they *were* slaves, in fact, to the Romans. Every third year their houses were ransacked and robbed by the Romans, and their wealth wrested from them. But, denying themselves all but the most necessary and coarsest food and raiment, in secret they constructed this grand temple, unknown to their lord the emperor. It was zeal that prompted the sacrifice, they believing it to be their first duty and moral obligation to erect a suitable temple for their deities."

We were off for Ismailia, a town on the Suez Canal. It is quite young, having been founded in 1863 to serve as a central point in the work on the canal. It is beautifully situated in the midst of gardens which are watered by canals conducting the water from the Nile. The journey through the desert between Cairo and Ismailia, in uncomfortably crowded cars, was not very pleasant. We passed over the battle-field, and saw the sand-hills beneath which many a brave English soldier sleeps who fell in the late war. But these men have not died in vain. They gave their lives that under God a new era might dawn in Egypt, and the sceptre of righteousness might reign in the land where the bigotry and superstition of the false prophet reigned too long.

From Ismailia we went to Port Said on a boat up the Suez Canal. The opening of this canal is one of the greatest works of the nineteenth century. It is eighty-six and one-half miles long, 250 feet wide, and of sufficient depth to allow the largest vessels to pass. About a month in time and from six to seven thousand miles in distance is thus saved between America or Europe and India and China. This canal was completed in 1863, at a cost of $130,000,000. From what we read in history, the cutting of this canal was no new scheme. Strabo says Rameses II. cut a canal between the Nile and the Red Sea thirteen centuries before Christ. Some say the work was done a century earlier, at the time Joseph was Governor. Herodotus says Necho II. enlarged this canal in the sixth century before Christ. He is said to have sacrificed more than 100,000 lives in the work. This canal was frequently repaired, but the Arab Caliphs, vandals that they were, entirely destroyed it. The canal of Napoleon III. extended from sea to sea, and although accomplished at so enormous an outlay of money, promises to pay itself. The revenue, which is annually increasing, amounts to $6,000,000 annually. The banks of the canal are very high. We who went up on a tug could only now and then catch a glimpse of the arid wastes beyond. It was the coldest ride I had in Egypt. The wind swept down the channel towards us with terrific violence; but the unpleasant voyage of over half the entire length, like all the unpleasant things in this life, came to an end, and an hour after dark we were at Port Said. This town, like that of Ismailia, came into being with the Suez Canal. It is about one hundred and fifty miles from Cairo, and by water not much farther from Alexandria. The land upon which it stands has been largely rescued from the sea. Large artificial stone protect the harbor from the inroads of the tides as they come and go. The population of the town is composed of almost every nationality under the sun. The French and the English predominate. This young city is not only the connecting link between Asia and Africa, it is in reality the stopping place between the great sea-ports of Europe and the Indian Ocean.

There are many marks of a higher civilization here. First of all, there is the "whisky shop." This alone is a proof that "civilized" people are here. The streets are wide, the houses are mostly frame, and on the whole the town resembles an American city in the west, more than anything I have seen whilst abroad. On the Sabbath we attended divine service in a neat and comfortable house belonging to the Church of England. We had a very pleasant Sabbath at Port Said.

It was about 4 p. m., when we embarked on a fine large German Lloyd steamer for Jaffa. The boat was literally covered with Mohammedan pilgrims. I had paid for a first cabin berth, but the cabin was crowded. I might have slept in the saloon, but the night being calm I preferred to wrap myself in blankets, and slept on a steamer chair on the promenade deck. Here I rested comfortably all night, and in the morning ate a hearty breakfast, whilst some who were in the "stuffy" cabin were far from comfortable. When the sun was up we anchored off Jaffa, the Joppa of the Bible.

I had been to Egypt, the land where Israel sojourned four hundred and thirty years, during which he became a great nation so that when he at last broke the shackles of bondage he went forth a great company, "six hundred thousand on foot that were men, besides children. And a mixed multitude went up also; and flocks even very much cattle." I had seen parts of the land of Goshen, the scenes of Israel's domestic tranquillity and barbarous oppression afterwards. I had, according to the best authorities, been within a few miles of Rameses, the capital or treasure city. In this place were discovered the remains of a magnificent palace, paved with alabaster, the walls of encaustic brick bearing inscriptions, and the oval of Rameses II. Though I had not left Egypt along the route which they took; I had no doubt crossed and recrossed their line of march on the way to the Red Sea. This route of Israel journeyings is now well defined by ash-heaps, the remains of their encampments over three thousand years ago, and by inscriptions found upon rocks. This is all very wonderful; but truth is ever stranger than fiction.

Such thoughts as these entered my mind on that calm night on the Mediterranean, as I looked up to the same stars at which Moses so often looked, as he led God's people from Egypt to the Land of Promise. It was with pleasure that I thought of the scenes which I was now to behold in that very land in which Israel dwelt after all his wanderings.

CHAPTER XIV.

JOPPA—Our arrival—Rolla Floyd—The "House by the seaside"—American convent—The school of Miss Arnot—Orange groves—Lutheran colony—Tropical garden—
ON THE ROAD TO JERUSALEM—Who all went this road—Flowers—Farming—Going to Market—Ramleh—Tower—Funeral—Dinner—View from the Mountains—Abou Gosch—Ain Karim—First View of Jerusalem.

IT was not long after the vessel came to anchor, before every one of our party was ready and eager to get ashore. We had arrived at seven o'clock, and anchored, as is usual, about half a mile outside of the city, which is built to the very edge of the Mediterranean. The distance from the ship to the shore is accomplished in small boats when the sea is not too wild. There are days when no landing can be effected; but this morning the sea was calm. A short time after our anchor was cast we were surrounded by a whole fleet of boats representing H. Gaze and Son, Thos. Cook and Son, and a few hotels. The Arab boatmen here as elsewhere make a loud noise by their discordant cries, in their eagerness to get everybody's attention. The crowding and pushing is something to be dreaded. But we were under the protection of Mr. Gaze himself, and the boats of Rolla Floyd, his agent, soon conveyed us safely to the shore, and through the much-dreaded Turkish custom-house. Mr. Floyd, by the way, is an American, a native of Maine ; but he has been in this country many years, and knows, it is said, every inch of the Holy Land better than any living dragoman. After a good breakfast we were ready for sight-seeing. Before we left the balcony of the hotel we saw a little lake which many years ago was connected with the sea. Here Hiram delivered his cedar logs to Solomon, which were used in the construction of the temple. From here they were transported over land, a distance of forty miles, to Jerusalem. We went to the " house by the sea side" where Peter saw the heavens opened, and "the Spirit said unto him, Behold, three men seek thee." We plucked a green fig from a tree standing in the yard, and some of the company took water from the old well where Peter used to quench his thirst. Whilst the house is not the same, the circumstances in connection with this wonderful vision, and the spreading of the Church of Christ, are all in favor of the site having been fully identified. Not far from the house of Simon the tanner is the place where Dorcas lived, and when she died, "full of good works and alms-deeds," her friends sent to Lydda for Peter, who came and restored her to life again.

We went to the Armenian convent, and entered the rooms in which Napoleon Bonaparte dwelt when in Joppa. From these rooms he issued his orders for the poisoning of five hundred of his countrymen, because he could not take them with him. This seemed very inhuman; but they would have fallen into the hands of the Turks, who would have murdered them in the most barbarous manner. The fact that this man here ordered four thousand Albian soldiers to be shot, after he had pledged his honor to treat them as prisoners of war, is far more atrocious, and without any excuse.

We turn away from these historic localities to a a spot which sheds not a little light and cheer amidst the filth and squalor and immorality of this region, under the influence and government of the Turk. We refer to the mission school of Miss Arnot. Here we saw about fifty girls, neat and clean: something so entirely different from the girls on the streets and in their wretched homes, that we almost felt at home. We heard them sing the same sweet Christian hymns we sing in our own loved land. This school was founded by Miss Arnot, in 1863, and though under the auspices of no society, has accomplished much good. Miss Arnot has a day school and a boarding school. Besides this there is an assembly of one hundred or more souls on the Sabbath for Protestant Christian worship. This school proves that missionary work among the degraded and ignorant women of the East pays far beyond all human expectation. It is by such work that the standard of the false prophet will eventually fall, and the banner of Christ will be made to wave over the land made sacred by His footsteps. As we looked into the bright, happy faces of these dear children, we resolved that if the Master spares us to return to our native land we will take more interest in Foreign Missions than ever before.

After leaving the mission school, we took a stroll through one of the large orange groves with which Joppa abounds. It is said fifty million oranges are picked in these groves every year. Most of them are sent to England. The fruit is larger, but not as sweet as some I have eaten from the groves around Cairo.

It may be interesting to us as Lutherans to

know that there is a colony of about three hundred souls in this place who came here from Wittenberg, who are an intelligent and active people. They have a neat little church which they call Lutheran, and a school for their children which is presided over by an "elder," who conducts the worship on the Sabbath.

Near the Lutheran colony is a beautiful tropical garden owned by a German Count whom I had the pleasure of meeting at Jerusalem. He saw us at the hotel in Joppa, and gave us a pressing invitation to call on him. His garden contains oranges, lemons and bananas. There are rose bushes here as tall as sour cherry trees, and geraniums six to ten feet high. The Count has a room in his palace filled with antiquities, gathered mostly from the Philistine country. Among these are pieces of statuary, household utensils, and many quaint and curious objects. The Count takes great pleasure in showing visitors around the beautiful garden, sweet with the perfume of orange blossoms, roses and other flowers.

Early on the next morning after our arrival in Joppa, we started for Jerusalem. After passing the the orange groves we came to the toll-gate. After getting our pass we were off along the old road to the Holy City. This is the old and the best road to be found in all Palestine. It was used in the days of Solomon. Along this road the cedars and other material for the building of the temple were brought, from Hiram king of Tyre. Along this road the Apostles passed to and from Joppa. Here too the Crusaders trod, as they went to deliver Jerusalem from the hands of the infidel. This road Joshua crossed and recrossed in the plain of Sharon. The first four or five miles after the traveler leaves Joppa he passes through orange and pomegranate groves, and olive orchards. It is early spring, and flowers bloom in abundance. Among them are the narcissus, the anemone, the lily and the tulip. We are on the plain of Sharon, and it is natural for us to look for the far-famed rose of Sharon. It is difficult to say which of the sweet-scented denizens of the plain is meant by Solomon when he says "I am the rose of Sharon." Some say it is a species of mallow. The flower generally pointed to by the dragoman has five petals, and is dark red, with a brown center; it grows about six inches high, and literally covers the plain.

On this plain we receive our first idea of Palestine farming. There is a peasant plowing with a heifer and a donkey unequally yoked together. Another has two oxen, which make much the better team. The plow consists of two poles which cross each other. The one passes to the yoke; the other forms a handle at one end, and to the other end a piece of iron as large as a good-sized garden hoe is attached. To drive his magnificent span, the plowman carries a spear six or eight feet long. The one end is pointed; the other has a sort of spade attached, with which he cleans the plowshare. The pointed end he uses to prod his team. It is a cruel stick, and recalls the words in Acts ix. 5—"It is hard for thee to kick against the goad." Looking at one of these goads, we can see how Shamgar could slay six hundred men with it. (Judges iii. 31.) There are no fences. Here and there a hedge surrounds an orchard. Fields and farms are marked by stones set on end. We can readily understand how Ruth could light in the field of Boaz apparently by mere chance.

Along the road we pass camels loaded with stones tied to each side of the faithful brute in a rope basket. We also pass donkeys and camels with oranges packed in the boxes, as we see them in our stores. Others have chickens in cages, or eggs packed with chaff in great baskets. The

Arabs make beasts of burden out of their wives and daughters. They carry everything imaginable in great loads upon their heads, whilst their lords drive camels or donkeys before them, or lounge lazily by the roadside.

Such scenes as these beguile the way. We are soon at Ramleh. This is said to be the place where Joseph of Arimathæa and Nicodemus were born. So the dragoman says; but, unfortunately, there is nothing to confirm the tradition. The streets of the town are very narrow and very dirty. There are plenty of dogs, lazy men and half-naked children to be seen. Just outside of the town, we saw a funeral. The body had just been put into the grave. A cluster of women in black gowns were sitting a little distance from the tomb, weeping and wailing. We would have thought that the deceased had many lady friends, had we not recalled what we learned in Sunday-school—namely that the mourners are hired here, and that the vehemence of their grief depends upon the amount of money received. At the grave itself there were many who had palm branches, the emblems of victory.

After we left Ramleh, we passed Gimzo, of 2 Chron. xxviii. 18, which the Philistines took from

Israel in the days of Ahab. We soon afterwards descended into the valley of Aijalon, where, "at the command of Joshua, the moon stayed until the people had avenged themselves upon their enemies."

When we came to Latrone, the reputed dwelling place of the penitent thief, we took dinner. There is a khan here owned by Rolla Floyd, to whom I have already referred. Travelers bring their lunch with them, and the men at the khan in the travelling season soon spread it on a nice clean cloth. The building itself, like all good buildings in this land of rocks, has thick stone walls, a stone porch, stone steps leading to second floor, which is of stone. It has a flat stone roof.

After an hour's rest we were again on the way. The road, which had already begun to ascend and and descend hills, now enters the mountains of Judea. There is little vegetation on the mountains. Low heath and a profusion of wild flowers grow among the rocks. Here and there we see a shepherd with a flock of goats or sheep, which run among the rocks and manage to find enough to sustain them. The road gradually winds up the mountain side until at last we are far above the plain of Sharon. Ramleh is in the distance. The road winds like a ribbon of silver over the limestone in the direction of Joppa ; and there beyond the stone towers rolls the Mediterranean. We now descend and are soon at Kirjath-jearim (now called Abou Gosch, after an Arab robber who formerly lived and did business here), where Abinadab kept the Ark of God for twenty years. There is nothing to be seen here except the ruins of a church, sometimes called the Church of Jeremiah. It is thought that this is the place where Jeremiah was born, the former name of Kirjath-jearim having been Anathoth. There are few who believe this. About forty-five minutes after we leave this town we reach the top of a hill from which we see the traditional burying-place of the prophet Samuel. In thirty minutes more we come to 'Ain Karim, surrounded by fig and olive orchards. Here it is said John the Baptist was born. In Luke i. 39 it is said, "Mary arose * * and went into the hill country with haste, into a city of Juda," which seems to be in favor of this place. At the foot of the hill is the dry bed of a brook from which David is said to have secured the stones with which he slew the Philistine giant. From this bridge which crosses the brook it is four miles to Jerusalem. The road winds gradually up the hill-side. Here, along these precipices, the Ark of God was brought and songs of joy were sung. But our journey is nearing its end. We hasten forward. Ascending a little hill by the side of the road, we get our first view of the Holy City. It is not the grand, the impressive view the traveler gains as he enters from the Mount of Olives on the other side of the city. The sun has already set, the shadows of evening are fallen, and we are soon at our hotel. We have gained the goal of our journey, and "hitherto the Lord has helped us."

CHAPTER XV.

IN THE HOLY CITY—First view—Temple plateau—Mosque of Omar—Sacred rock—El Aksa—"Solomon's Stables"—Via Dolorosa—Hospice, Convent of St. John—Church of Holy Sepulchre—Anointing slab—Where Mary stood—Sepulchre Where Crosses were, etc.—House of Caiaphas—Where the "cock crew"—Supper room—Tomb of David, Church of St. Anne—Bethesda—General description of City.

AFTER a good night's rest we were up bright and early to have our first walk in Jerusalem. One can scarcely give vent to his feelings as he is about for the first time to enter the Holy City, the fountain from which civilization has taken its source. It is remarkable that on the banks of the muddy Tiber there should have arisen the Forum and the Palace of the Cæsars, the synonyms for a civilization which in the days of its greatest glory pervaded the then known world. It is even more wonderful, that the threshing floor of Ornan, on Mt. Moriah, should be made an altar on which was offered the Sacrifice, "which taketh away the sins of the world"—that Sacrifice which, in the very act of being offered, has robbed death of its

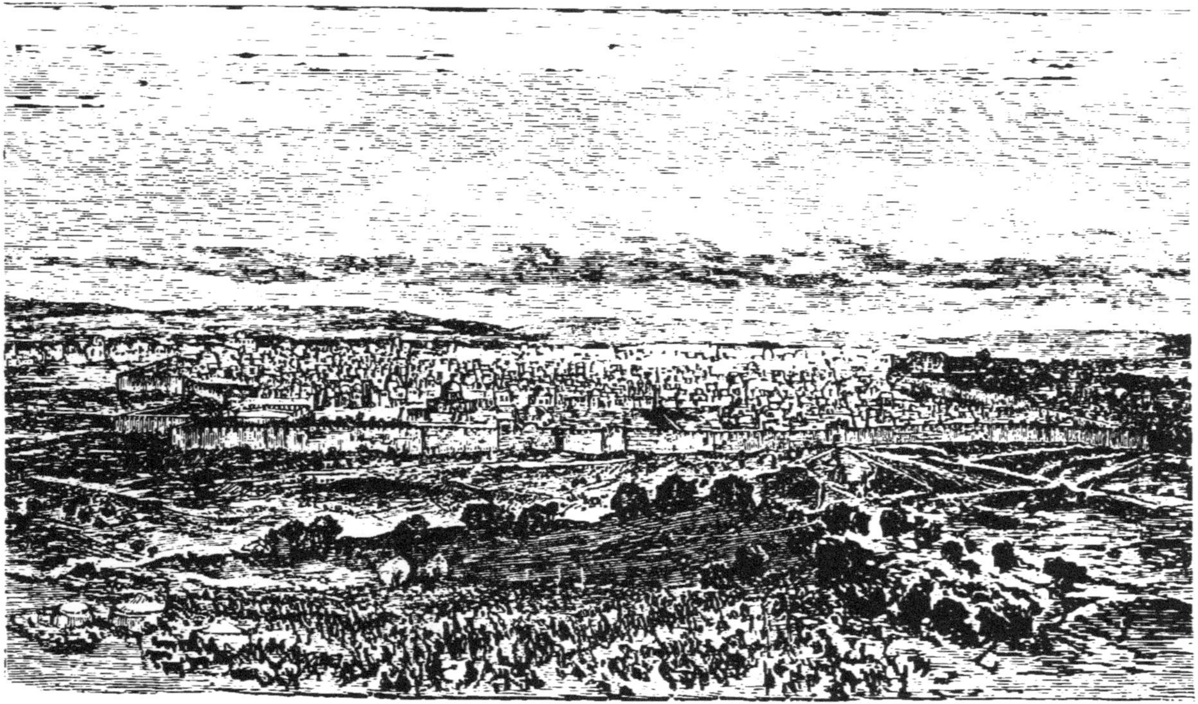

JERUSALEM FROM OLIVET.

Page 208

sting and the grave of its victory, and laid the foundations of a new development, greater and grander than that which originated on the banks of the muddy Tiber, or the sandy Nile. This Jerusalem Christ hallowed by His footsteps, and made it sacred by His blood, thus constituting it the centre from which should emanate the energizing power which has quickened humanity into a new life, and has given it the hope of a glorious immortality.

I caught my first glimpse of the Holy City from the northwest, where the traveler sees Russian buildings outside the walls and the dome of the Mosque of Omar on the temple plateau. The better view is from the Mount of Olives. There one sees the gray old wall on the east, with the Gate of St. Stephen, always open now, and the Golden Gate, closed for centuries already. Here the Mosque of Omar and the Mosque of El Aksa stand in bold relief. West of these the domes of the church of the Holy Sepulchre are seen. The half dozen towers which are prominent in the different parts of the city are minarets, from which the muezzin is sounded at dawn, near noon, in the afternoon, a little after sunset, and at nightfall. There is a similarity of architecture throughout the city which is exceedingly monotonous. One sees straight walls, some of them higher, some of them lower. These walls contain few windows. The roofs are flat. Some of them have a dome-like centre, as if a great ball made of stone stuck part of the way above the roof. I have seen men sitting on some of these roofs smoking their pipes, and blinking like great owls on the crowd below.

If the traveler enters by the St. Stephen's Gate, and has provided himself with a pass and a Turkish soldier, he generally turns his face toward the Mosque of Omar. On his way he passes the Jews' wailing-place. This is a wall 150 feet long and 50 feet high, and of great age. If it is Friday afternoon, Jews from every country of the civilized world may be seen standing with their faces toward the wall, chanting in Hebrew such parts of the Bible as the 79th Psalm and the 64th chapter of Isaiah. The old wall is full of rusty nails, which the Jews leave, thinking that this memorial of their having been there secures them the forgiveness of their sins.

The Temple plateau, upon which the Mosque of Omar stands, is an irregular quadrangle almost a mile around. Much of it is artificial in its construction, and is a marvel in itself. We entered the mosque on the east, after having taken off our shoes, as the Mohammedans compel you to do at the entrance of all their mosques. The Mosque of Omar is an octagon 536 feet in circumference. The dome is 97 feet high. Many of the marble columns are curiously wrought, and together with many of the slabs in the side of the building, came no doubt from Solomon's temple. The light comes through richly-stained glass windows placed at the top where the dome begins. In the centre of the building is the bare native rock. This rock has the most wonderful history of any on the face of the earth. Here, it is believed, Abraham laid Isaac bound and ready for the sacrifice. Here Ornan had his threshing floor when the angel appeared. Here David built an altar and offered burnt offerings. Here was the Holy of Holies in that greatest and grandest temple ever dedicated to God. Here man's hand has thrown down and destroyed the most sacred edifices; but this rock is here, as it was in the days of Abraham.

The Mohammedans have surrounded this rock with their own superstitions. They say from this rock Mahomet ascended to heaven. They show you the finger-marks of the angel Gabriel, who seized upon the rock to keep it from going with the false prophet. In confirmation of this tradition the traveler is shown the cave beneath the rock. They declare the rock is suspended in the air. Of course the sides where the rock rests are carefully concealed with plaster. In this cave Ornan and his four sons no doubt hid themselves when they saw the angel of the Lord. (1 Chron. xxi. 20.)

At the entrance to the cave the guide points to a hole in the rock in which, properly concealed, are three hairs of the false prophet's beard. There were more originally, but the devil, say they, stole the others!

There is a jasper slab in the floor to the north side of the mosque. If you put money on this slab you will be sure of going to heaven! In this stone were nineteen golden nails. An angel has taken all but three away. When the last nail is gone, the world will come to an end!

There is much in and about this holy place to be seen and contemplated. When the full light of day streams through the fifty-six gorgeous windows, the place is bathed in an almost unearthly splendor. I visited this mosque twice, and each time my reverence for the place increased. Leaving the mosque by the south door, where Christ had the conversation with regard to the tribute money, (Matt. xxii. 17-22,) we are on the temple porch. Beneath this are immense cisterns and caverns. Who knows what relics of the ancient temple may yet lie concealed here? Perhaps the Ark of the Covenant is there somewhere. There is no satisfactory proof that it was ever carried away. A few years ago the seal of Haggai, who was divinely commissioned more than 500 B. C. to restore the Lord's house, was found on a hill at the southern extremity of the temple platform.

At the southern end of the Haram enclosure is a mosque which is supposed to have been built by Justinian in honor of the Virgin. It is now called the Mosque of El Aksa. This mosque is a large structure and is famous chiefly for its heterogeneous material, some of which is very beautiful, and some very ordinary. Most of the columns here are no doubt from Solomon's temple. Many of them are now covered with plaster. Near the entrance to the mosque are the reputed tombs of Aaron's sons. Close to these tombs is a well which once afforded an entrance to Paradise to a man who went down. He brought with him a golden leaf and gave a wonderful account of what he saw, so the Mohammedans say. In the southeast part of the temple platform is the entrance to an interesting place. Descending a flight of thirty-two steps we are shown the cradle of Christ, where it is said the infant Redeemer was laid after his presentation in the temple. Going a few steps farther we are in what is called "Solomon's stables." There are no less than one hundred piers of solid masonry which support the arches above them. Into the edges of many of the piers holes were bored, through which the Crusaders slipped their hitching-straps and tied their horses. Solomon never used the place for a stable. It may be that the whole structure was erected to support the temple porch above. That the inhabitants of Jerusalem frequently sought shelter here in times of siege, can hardly be doubted. In this place the conduit through which the blood of the sacrifice was washed into the Kedron is seen. In the southeast is a stone which had evidently been cut for a place in the temple; but for some reason it was thrown aside. It was afterwards placed into the corner of this structure. It is no doubt to this stone that Christ refers when he says, "The stone which the builders rejected, the same is become the head of the corner." (Matt. xxi. 42f.; Ps. cxviii. 22.)

After leaving the temple area we come to the place where the houses of the Levites stood.

The better way from the Mosque of Omar to the church is by a gate opening on a narrow street, which leads past what was formerly supposed to be the Pool of Bethesda. This so-called Pool of Bethesda is almost seventy feet lower than the Haram south of it. The place is rapidly being filled up with garbage, which emits an intolerable stench. This pool was probably supplied by water from the pools of Solomon, and never had any water of its own. It is more than probable that this pool once formed a moat for the Tower of Antonia, which stood beside it. It was from this tower that Paul addressed the mob after he had been rescued by the chief captain (Acts xxi. 30-40; xxii.)

Quite near this place the *Via Dolorosa* begins. This is supposed to be the street along which Christ bore the cross from Pilate's judgment hall to Golgotha. Fourteen sacred places are pointed out, all of which are connected with that awful journey. At one place a picture of Christ is shown on the wall. Here it is said St. Veronica gave her kerchif to Christ to wipe his face; when she again received it, there was an exact image of Christ's sorrowful face on it. This handkerchief is still in the possession of the Roman Catholic Church!

At another place the spot where Christ sank to the ground beneath the weight of the cross is pointed out—then, further on, the spot where the cross was laid on Simon.

Far more interesting is the Catholic convent, in the chapel of which a very old arch is shown. On this arch Christ is said to have stood when Pilate said, "Behold the man." Whether this is the very arch is not certain; but it is more probable that this was the arch than the one outside, spanning the street. The convent in itself is interesting, in as much as it forms an oasis of cleanliness in a veritable desert of filth. The bright girls in the orphanage are taught all the customs and usefulness of civilized life. The fancy work of these little ones and of the Sisters who have them in training is very fine.

Outside of the court of the Church of the Holy Sepulchre, are the ruins of the Hospice of the Knights of St. John. This was a vast structure, the greater part of which is in ruins. The stone buildings were constructed around a great open square. The second story of one wing of the large building is now used as a Lutheran church. On Easter Sabbath morning I heard the sweetest singing in this church I ever heard anywhere.

The song was led by the orphan girls from the German Protestant home, "Talithi-Cumi." This church is attended by all German residents in the city, and by many visitors. The pastor delivered a short, impressive and edifying sermon on Christ's resurrection. What made it doubly impressive was the fact that the event occurred near the spot where the preacher addressed us. About a dozen of the dark-eyed, red-cheeked little girls who sang, united with the church. I felt sure that if I could have had my congregation away in America look upon that Eastern scene, and then could have taken them to some home to behold the filth and learn the ignorance in which Mohammedan children are brought up, it would have preached them an eloquent missionary sermon.

In the court of this church one can see portions of beautiful marble columns and capitals which are very old, perhaps from Solomon's temple, but the tooth of time has had little effect upon them. The hammer of the Vandal has done much more to deface them. The vast cisterns beneath the courts and ruins no doubt contain some things of interest; but so far as I know they have never been explored.

Leaving these grand old ruins, we step into the court of the most renowned church in Jerusalem. In front of the Church of the Holy Sepulchre is a court which is always filled with men, women and children who sell glass beads, olive wood beads, glass bracelets, ivory and wooden crosses, combs, tapers and flowers. The building itself was erected in the 11th century by the Crusaders. It was partly destroyed by fire in 1808. The present edifice is 230 feet wide from east to west, and 200 feet long from north to south.

The first object of interest is the Anointing Slab, a piece of yellowish marble upon which Nicodemus anointed Christ prior to his putting him into his own new tomb. Pilgrims measure this stone and make their winding-sheets the same length. Not far from this stone, under an iron frame, is a round marble stone where Mary stood when Christ said "Woman, behold thy son: Son, behold thy mother." Immediately under the great dome, which is 65 feet in diameter, is the Holy Sepulchre. It is of white marble, and is 26 feet long by 17 feet wide by 15 feet high. Outside are dozens of silver censers. Besides these I saw on Palm Sunday scores of tapers, all burning, producing a pleasing effect on the dim and smoky looking surroundings. An oil painting of the risen Christ is suspended immediately above the opening to the sepulchre. The chamber within is 16 feet long by 10 feet wide. This room is lighted by fifteen silver lamps—five belonging to the Latins, five to the Greeks, four to the Armenians, and one to the Copts. Here they show you a portion of the stone which the women found rolled away. Passing through a low door so narrow that only one at a time can enter, we come into a room 6 feet by 6. This is the *sanctum sanctorum* of the place. This is lighted by lamps of solid gold. A slab covers the real rock, in which is the reputed tomb of our Lord. Through a rent in the marble slab the holy fire comes on the Greek Easter. The slab is worn by millions of kisses which have been showered upon it.

Not far from this sepulchre, in a dilapidated old chapel belonging to the Copts, are two very old Jewish tombs, which I must confess I approached and examined with more reverence than the chapel of the reputed sepulchre. To the west is a marble slab where Mary is said to have stood when she said to Jesus, supposing him to be a gardener, "Sir if thou have borne him hence, tell me where thou hast laid him." In a chapel to the north of the sepulchre and fifteen feet above it are several chapels. In the largest of these is a natural rock. In this rock is a silver socket, in which the cross is said to have rested. About five feet to the right and the same distance to the left, the position of the other two crosses is seen. The rock which was rent by the earthquake is here, too. In an iron grating is the marble pillar to which Christ was chained when he was scourged. Pilgrims take a long stick and touch this pillar, then kiss the end of the stick. The place where the cross was found, and the rock on which the Empress Helena sat watching the excavators in search of the cross, and from whence she threw coins to the workmen, is also shown. In short, the Church of the Holy Sepulchre is a regular museum. Yet Christ may have been buried in one of these old tombs. That He was likewise crucified here is scarcely credible.

One of the most sacrilegious farces which used to be enacted here, is now, by law, discontinued. I refer to the custom of receiving holy fire on the Greek Easter. The church used to be thronged on these occasions. The Greek Patriarch would, at the proper time, pass a lighted torch out of an elliptical hole in the marble wall of the Chapel of the Angels. This fire, it was claimed, was supernatural and came from the empty tomb. The pilgrims would light their torches and burn their clothing, and scorch their hands, hoping to merit favor thereby from their risen Lord.

Passing southward along Christian street, we go out Zion Gate. Not far from Zion Gate is the Armenian monastery, which is said to cover the site of the house of Caiaphas. Here they show you the footprints of the cock that crew (!) when Peter denied his Lord. The place where Peter stood is pointed out with the utmost precision ! Not far from this is the place where Christ is said to have instituted the Holy Communion. They show you the very table which was used on the occasion. No one believes these lies, but it is well to mention that these fellows have unbounded confidence in the credulity of pilgrims and tourists.

Here is the tomb of David. There is very little doubt that the ashes of more than a dozen of Israel's illustrious kings sleep near here. The "Castle of Zion" was the royal residence of David, and when he died "he was buried in the city of David." (1 Kings ii, 10). When Nehemiah was rebuilding the walls of the city he refers to the sepulchres of David (Nehemiah iii. 15 and 16). From the writings of Cyril, Bishop of Jerusalem, it is learned that a Christian Church once stood here. The foundations of this building are very ancient. The stones have the Jewish bevel, and are held together with stone knobs and sockets. Over the reputed tomb is an upper room to which visitors are admitted. This is the room I have mentioned as the place where the Holy Supper was instituted. Here, too, the Holy Ghost is said to have come upon the disciples on the day of Pentecost. The tradition is nearly as old as the Christian religion.

This is a sacred locality, and carefully guarded by the Turks. Dr. De Hass speaks of having entered the crypt beneath the room described.* In this crypt is a door with an oval top. The Turks say persons who attempted to enter here were struck with blindness. In consequence, the door was walled shut many years ago. There is an Arabic inscription over the door saying, "This is the gate to heaven." Some day that masonry will be taken down, and who knows what mysteries the space beyond may reveal!

This brief description of sacred places would be entirely too incomplete, were I not to mention the

---

*"Buried Cities," p. 178.

Church of St. Ann, and the Pool of Bethesda behind it. This church was built in honor of the mother of the Virgin Mary in the time of the Crusaders. The church stands in a court (a yard we Americans would say) which is adorned with flowers and piles of broken columns and statuary found in the excavations. Going down 21 steps, the traveler is in the crypt, where the Virgin is said to have been born. The church belongs to the Roman Catholics, and is furnished with movable chairs and benches.

Far more interesting is the Pool of Bethesda, a few rods to the west. It is without doubt the pool of which the Evangelist speaks. (John v. 2.) The pool is now deep down in the earth. The lowest masonry is of Jewish origin. Above this is Roman masonry; then the Crusaders built an arch above this, and lastly the Turks. Below it all is the water. The remains of the five porches are to be seen. Standing on the lowest level, I felt almost confident that I stood where Christ once stood, and where He manifested the power of God in healing the impotent man.

I must close this chapter by reminding the reader that the glory of Jerusalem is in its ruins, and not in the achievements of its present people.

Everywhere within the walls in its present places of interest, and beyond the walls on the Mount of Olives, in its tombs, its pools, and even in the countless mosaics which lie scattered over the soil for miles around Jerusalem, is written the story of its ancient greatness. In these ruins is recorded the fact that the city lies low but mighty in the dust.

The streets of the present Jerusalem are narrow as they no doubt always were. Immediately within the Jaffa gate, around the tower of David, which is now a citadel as it always was, and the foundations of which date back to the time of Israel's greatest monarch, there is a beautiful open place, and the street running south is wide. Here on this place the American Consul has his office, but we never found him in.

The two principal thoroughfares are David's street and Christian street. They are so narrow that two buggies could not pass each other.

The Turkish post-office is on David's street. It looks like a second class barber-shop. The postmaster hands you all the letters to let you see if there is anything for you. As soon as the mail comes in, he sends European and American letters to Bergenheimer's, the banker's.

One sees no vehicles of any kind on the streets. Now and then a "ship of the desert" strides majestically along. The quick and sure-footed little donkey brings his load of vegetables or a few dead sheep on his back to the markets. The markets are kept in bazaars or niches of the houses, and on the streets. Peasants come from the surrounding country with onions, leeks, salads, potatoes, eggs, chickens, olives, almonds and sheep. They crowd the narrow streets and jabber and gesticulate from morning to night.

There are bazaars filled with very fine goods. The olive wood curiosities are very pretty. Almost every thing imaginable is made out of olive wood and sold here as souvenirs. The articles made of mother of pearl are also very fine, but Bethlehem is the headquarters for all mother of pearl goods.

CHAPTER XVI.

A walk about Zion—View from Olivet—Mosque of the Ascension—"Czar's Church"—Gethsemane—Virgin's Tomb—The Kedron—Absalom's Pillar—Tombs—Enrogel—Pools of Gihon—Quarries of Solomon—Golgotha—Church of St. Stephen—Tombs of the Kings—Tombs of the Judges—King's Winepresses—Land of Wonders.

THERE was more to be seen to impress the beholder with the beauty and grandeur of the places and objects about the Holy City when Solomon sat upon the throne of Israel than now; but a walk about Zion is of interest in our own day. The best place from which to view the environments of Jerusalem is from the Russian observatory on the summit of Olivet. The top of this tower is 3000 feet above the level of the sea. The view is sublime. To the east you look over a stretch of barren mountains and deep waddies into the Jordan valley. The Jordan glistens like a ribbon of silver (where the vegetation on its banks does not hide the water) as it winds on its way to the Dead Sea. And there, stretching away to the south like a great mass of dark blue sky come down to earth, is the Dead Sea. From one of those mountain peaks which border the sea, Moses looked upon the Promised Land. At the extreme north of the view of the valley, one sees the site of ancient Jericho, that monument placed by the power of God to the triumphs of faith. To the west you look down upon Jerusalem; whilst beyond you see the road as it winds toward Joppa. To the north you see the road that leads to Damascus. Almost immediately in front of Olivet is the hill from which Titus first beheld the city, when he began that memorable siege in which a million Jews perished, and the Holy City was razed to its foundations.

We descend the tower, and on going down the mount we come first to the place from which Christ is said to have ascended to heaven. You enter a court-yard through a gate. In the yard there is a Mohammedan prayer-house built over a rock from which Christ arose. The foot-print of the Saviour is shown on the rock. The Arabs are there to collect *backshish*, and for them the place has as much interest as if Christ had really ascended from the spot, which is doubted by the best critics.

The new Russian church built by the Czar is not far from the place of the Ascension. The church is the finest modern place of worship in Palestine.

It is a Greek mosque, and is noted for its paintings, rich robes and altar drapings. In excavating for the foundations of this church, skulls, tear bottles, and bottles which once contained perfumery or anointing oil, were found. These curiosities are carefully preserved and shown to visitors. What astonished me more than the architecture of the building or its fine furnishings was the fact that the polite sexton refused *backshish*. He is the only man in Palestine who refused *backshish*. We had, however, scarcely gotten out of the church before an Arab wanted to show us down the hill, but we knew the way as well as he. Then he wished to bring us a drink, but we refused; then he called for *backshish*. When you pass these people on the street they ask you for *backshish*. When they see you at a distance they come holding out their hands crying *backshish*.

At the foot of Olivet is the garden of Gethsemane. Just outside the gate there are three flat rocks, which are pointed out as the places where the three disciples slept whilst Jesus prayed. A broken column at the gate is said to mark the spot where Judas betrayed his Master with a kiss. The garden itself is surrounded by a picket fence. Inside this fence is a pebble walk about six feet wide.

Then there is an iron fence, beyond which are roses and other pretty flowers. In the square enclosed by the iron fence are eight old olives, one of which is nineteen feet in circumference. These trees are no doubt from the roots of those which stood in the time of Christ. I say, "from the roots," because Josephus says Titus destroyed *all* the trees. The article in the *Sunday-school Times* published recently, trying to prove that this *cannot* be the site of Gethsemane, makes much ado about nothing. Whilst this may not be the precise spot of our Lord's agony, it can not be far removed. What a place this garden is for holy thoughts and renewed consecration to the Master's service! It was here somewhere that the seen and unseen worlds met. Here was worked out man's salvation, and on Calvary it was finished. Here angels "sweetly soothed the Saviour's woe," after the awful contest with the powers of darkness.

After leaving the garden of Gethsemane, we go nearly due north about one hundred yards to the Virgin's tomb. Several flights of steps lead down a distance of thirty-five feet into a chapel cut out of solid rock. This chapel is eighteen feet wide and ninety feet long. It is illuminated with dozens of solid silver lamps. Here the tomb of the parents of the Virgin is to be seen. Near this tomb is a sarcophagus which is said to contain the ashes of Mary. There is a spring of water in the tomb, which in itself is almost a miracle in this country. Whether the ashes of those mentioned really repose here, no one knows and few care, but it is an interesting place to visit.

We are now in the valley of the Kedron. In the days of Christ the ravine was much deeper. Captain Warren, of the "Palestine Exploration Fund," discovered the original channel of the Kedron eighty feet below the surface. No wonder Josephus said that it made one dizzy to stand upon the wall of Jerusalem and look down into the ravine below. The height is still great, but not so great as it was before the debris of the thrice-destroyed city was gathered in the valley. Looking down the Kedron valley we see the tomb of Absalom. This is a cube about twenty feet high, surmounted by a pyramid of solid stone about ten feet high. The whole is cut out of the solid native rock. The chamber inside is nearly full of stones, thrown there out of contempt of the ashes said to repose within. This is without doubt the place where the rebellious son was buried, and over these rocks David clambered when he fled from Jerusalem.

Further south are three other remarkable tombs, respectively called the tomb of Jehoshaphat, the grotto of St. James, and the tomb of Hezekiah. The first two are excavations in the solid rock, the front being ornamented by a cornice, also cut out of the same rock. The tomb of Hezekiah resembles that of Absalom. The whole hillside opposite the city is a burial place for the Jews. They come here to die and to be buried from almost every land, because they think the Messiah, when he comes, will enter the city from this hill, and first raise the dead here. The well of Job, at the extreme end of the Kedron valley, is the only well in all this district of country. The Pool of Siloam, to which Christ sent the blind man to wash, is south of Jerusalem, at the point where the Tyropean valley enters that of the Kedron. Remnants of the old wall, which was doubtless put there in the time of David, are still to be seen. The larger and lower pool is almost filled with stones and rubbish.

The valley of Hinnom comes down from the west of Jerusalem, and unites at Enrogel with the Kedron. Here is the place where Adonijah, when David was old, made a great feast for the king's servants and men of Judah (1 Kings, i. 9). The valley of Hinnom is the *Gehenna* in which they burned the rubbish. It divides Mount Zion from the Hill of Evil Counsel. Upon this hill, it is said, the dwelling of Caiaphas stood, where he took counsel with the Jews how he might put Jesus to death—hence the name Evil Counsel. Half way up the hill is the "Field of Blood," bought with the "thirty pieces of silver."

In this valley, southwest from Jerusalem, is the lower Pool of Gihon. It is forty feet deep, and covers nearly three acres of ground. It was capable of holding nineteen million gallons of water. The water was probably used for the gardens which once abounded in this valley. The upper Pool of Gihon is about a quarter of a mile west of the Joppa Gate. This pool is smaller than the other, and not half as deep. It was close to this pool that Zadok and Nathan anointed Solomon king of Israel.

Leaving these wonderful ruins on the west, we bend our steps nearly due northeast toward the Damascus Gate, so called because the road from Damascus enters the Holy City by this gate. A little to the northeast of this gate is a small door in the hillside. In 1852 Dr. Barclay's dog disappeared in this opening. One night Dr. Barclay and his two sons entered this opening with candles and cords and solved what had been a mystery for years, the question as to where Solomon obtained his stones for the temple. The quarry is 3000 feet in circumference, and in some places is thirty feet deep. The chippings of the ancient workmen are still here. So are the black marks of their torches on the ceiling. It is estimated that enough stone has been taken out of these quarries to build two Jerusalems. The stone is white as chalk and very soft, but hardens on exposure to the sun. Free Masons claim that their noble order originated in these caverns among Solomon's masons. The manner in which these ancient masons cut the stone is seen. They had an instrument like an adz with which they cut a groove into the rocks, then they put a wooden wedge into the groove and wetted it. This caused the wedge to swell and burst the rock from its bed. There was an opening near the temple through which the stones were lifted. The quarries are opposite the grotto of Jeremiah, where the prophet is said to have written that wonderful book, some of the sayings of which are even now being fulfilled. Above the grotto is a Mohammedan cemetery. The highest and most rugged point is believed to be the spot where the Son of God was crucified. This answers the Evangelists' description, and is no doubt the place.

To the northeast of the city is the newly excavated church of St. Stephen. A few years ago a poor Greek was excavating here for a new house, when he came upon a beautiful mosaic floor. The Roman Catholic church paid him $10,000 for the lot, and continued the excavation. They laid bare the floor of an immense church, which must have been erected before the days of the Crusaders. Underneath are tombs having Christian emblems, similar to those seen in the catacombs at Rome. Here are seen stone doors with stone hinges, and great round stones, which were rolled before the door, as in the days of Christ. Who knows but that St. Stephen was stoned and then reverently interred on the site marked by this ancient edifice?

The so-called "Tombs of the Kings" are about half a mile north from the Damascus Gate. These tombs were discovered in digging a cistern. The workmen came upon a large stone coffin containing human remains. This coffin stood in the midst of a vast chamber hewn out of the solid rock. There was no name upon it, but it is said to have contained valuable jewels. Near this place, as we have just learned in this chapter, once stood the grand church of St. Stephen. The beautiful Eudocia, wife of Theodosius II., died here. The remains in the sarcophagus may have been those of the unfortunate queen, or of the martyred Stephen himself.

The tomb is enclosed in a yard with a high board fence. We knocked at the gate, when a woman opened from within, and after giving us tapers we went down a flight of broad stone steps into a large chamber. In the centre was a large cistern—at least the room was filled with water. Turning to the left we entered the chamber where the sarcophagus was found. From the main chamber there are passages leading into many smaller rooms or crypts. The passages into these are narrow and low, and it is with difficulty that the tourist gains entrance. There are four smaller chambers in all. The bodies were laid on niches, or shelves, cut out of the rock. Others were inserted, as loaves are put into an oven. These openings were closed with stones and sealed. The entire tomb must at one time have contained 75 bodies. The tomb may have been constructed during successive generations, inasmuch is it was easy to cut successive chambers even after the dead were deposited in the first chamber. This is altogether the largest and finest rock-hewn tomb I saw in Palestine.

About a mile northwest from this tomb is another which is known as the "Tombs of the Judges." The outside of this tomb is decorated with a cornice cut into the face of the rock. The vestibule is twelve feet wide, and is ornamented with vines and flowers and figures. The place is often used as a shelter for Bedouin Arabs. Their fires have blackened the walls. Here, as at the Tombs of the Kings, there is one large chamber (about twenty feet square) from which there are entrances into the smaller chambers or vaults. It is very probable that those who once judged Israel, before Saul was anointed king, slept for many years here. The hand of the Vandal long since scattered their ashes and carried off the treasures which were buried with them. Truly they have brought out "the bones of his princes, and the bones of the priests, and the bones of the prophets, and the bones of the inhabitants of Jerusalem out of their graves," and have "spread them before the sun."

Not far from the Tombs of the Judges is the "King's Wine-press." This is the king's wine-press to which Zechariah refers in his prophecy, and of which the next chapter of this volume treats. The wine-presses were cut into the solid rock. Here the grapes were trodden in the times of vintage more than twenty-three centuries ago. The large stone vats are to be seen where the juice fermented. Near by are the immense cisterns in which the wine was stored. The whole establishment, vats, cisterns and all, is cut out of the solid rock, and is a marvel of ancient workmanship.

This whole country is a land of wonders and sacred associations. In this land, among these people, God prepared a religion for mankind which is more enduring than these rock-hewn tombs, and the blessings of which are being inherited by the nations which were as yet unborn when these tombs were new. God grant that these people, the ashes of whose ancestors repose here, may ere long be led to receive Him as their Saviour, whom their fathers rejected. Then this country, we firmly believe, will once more blossom as the rose.

CHAPTER XVII.

Fulfilment of Prophecy—Spirit of Improvement in the City—Industrial School—Jeremiah xxxii. 38-40—The New Jerusalem—Zechariah xiv. 10—Characteristics of the New Town—Conversion of Jews.

IN walking about Jerusalem one is impressed with the fact that at last the spirit of progress is being felt in the Holy City. Sewers are being dug, new streets are being opened, and new buildings, many of them possessing all the modern improvements, are being erected. It will not be long before the shriek of the locomotive will be heard on the plains of Sharon and in the mountains of Judea, as it brings the comforts, the commerce, and the pilgrims of the civilized nations "up to the mountain of the Lord."

If the spirit of improvement is seen within the walls, it is still more manifest beyond those walls. There is literally a new Jerusalem going up outside the walls. Beginning at the Jaffa gate and extending along the Jaffa road for a mile, it widens on the first eminence beyond the upper pool of Gihon into a beautiful town. The houses in this new town are larger and much more comfortable than those in the old city. The streets are wider, and the blocks of buildings are in regular squares. Here and there a stone wall is seen enclosing rows of trees, which will in a few years develop into shady parks. The inhabitants of this new town, though Jews, are different from those who dwell in the "Jews' Quarter," in filth and poverty, on Mount Zion, within the walls of the city. On the Jaffa road there is a large industrial school, where the Jewish youths are taught any trade to which they may incline. This new Jerusalem will have first-class mechanics of every description. There are no less than ten such colonies in Palestine to-day, and of all these none is more flourishing than the colony at Jerusalem. Rothschild and those who are assisting him are doing a good work among their countrymen.

But is not this development of the country, and this lifting of the Jews, under the guiding hand of the God of nations? Is He not fulfilling the promises made unto the fathers many centuries ago? In the reign of Zedekiah, more than five centuries before Christ, the Lord causes Jeremiah to say: "Behold the days come, saith the Lord, that the city (referring to Jerusalem) shall be built to the

Lord from the tower of Hananeel unto the gate of the corner, and the measuring line shall yet go out straight onward unto the hill Gareb and shall turn about unto Goah. And the whole valley of the dead bodies, and of the ashes, and all the fields, unto the brook Kedron, unto the corner of the horse gate toward the east, shall be holy unto the Lord; it shall not be plucked up, nor thrown down any more for ever." Jer. xxxi. 38–40. In all the rebuildings of the city after the successive destructions by Chaldean, Roman and Turk, the words of the prophet were never fulfilled. The new city which we have briefly described follows in its construction the district indicated by the prophet. Only a year or two ago, when the foundations for the "New Hotel," near the Joppa gate, where being dug, the workmen came upon the top of an old tower. There is good reason for supposing this to be the tower of Hananeel. The ancient hill Gareb is west of Jerusalem. It is upon this hill that the substantial and comfortable houses we have mentioned are erected. The "valley of the dead bodies" is distinctly marked by tombs of undoubted antiquity, and is in direct line of these modern improvements. It is to this same rebuilding of Jerusalem that Zechariah refers (in the xiv.

chapter and 10th verse of his prophecy) when he says: "It shall be lifted up, and inhabited in her place, from Benjamin's gate unto the place of the first gate, unto the corner gate, and from the tower of Hananeel unto the king's wine-presses." The king's wine-presses were discovered a few years ago, not far from the Tomb of the Judges. The buildings of this new city will no doubt in a few years cover this place even "unto the ashes." "The ashes" refers to the ashes of the sacrifices, which, according to Levit. vi. 11, were carried forth by the priest to a clean place without the camp. When the sacrifices were no longer offered in the tabernacle, the law was observed by carrying them, after the manner prescribed, beyond the city walls. There were two places to which these ashes were transported. Some years ago these ashes formed immense heaps. One of these is now entirely used up in the making of mortar, and the place is covered with new buildings. The other is fully identified, to the north of the Damascus gate, and is also rapidly disappearing. At the present rate of building, it will not be many years before the new city covers every foot of the territory described by the prophets mentioned. The places of the ancient gates mentioned are not easily identified, but the other landmarks are determined by a precision which admits of no doubt.

This new city is characterized by the fact that "it shall not be plucked up, nor thrown down any more forever." The city, which has often been overthrown, is now built to remain. The Jew who returns to this new Jerusalem in the land of his fathers, needs fear no captivity. There shall be no besieging armies. The gates of the city shall be open continually: "they shall not be shut day nor night." Christ will be King there; but the manner of His presence is, we think, not revealed.

The land in the districts described, with little exception, belongs to the Jews, and more of it is being purchased by them every year. This land is paid for by individuals or societies, and is secured to the purchaser by the necessary legal documents. All this is in strict accordance with what Jeremiah says: "Men shall buy fields for money and subscribe the deeds, and seal them, and call witnesses, in the land of Benjamin and in the places about Jerusalem," etc. Jer. xxxii. 44. It is not many years since lands were bought and sold in this way, and this simple business transaction is in itself a striking fulfillment of prophecy.

Everybody knows that the Jews are returning in

large numbers to this, the home of their fathers. The fact is frequently commented upon, but the full extent of this ingress is not realized by those who live thousands of miles from Jerusalem. In 1882, for the first time since the captivity, two hundred of the tribe of Gad came to Jerusalem.*

They were in extreme poverty, and were befriended by Christian missionaries in Jerusalem. One of those who saw them and helped them, told me that they could give no reason for their coming other than they felt a strong and unaccountable incentive to come. The first party numbered only one hundred and fifty; now there are nearly one thousand of them in the new city; and what is more, many of them have homes of their own. These, and their brethren, are rapidly displacing other nationalities in Jerusalem. Formerly no Jew was allowed to transact business in the Holy City.

The question arises, how can Palestine support a dense population with its bare and unproductive mountains? The soil is literally washed from the hillsides by the rains of centuries, leaving the bare rocks to glare in the sunlight. The narrow valleys are fertile. The whole plain of Jericho could

---

*I am indebted to the "Americans" for some facts herein mentioned.

be made productive, if it were properly irrigated from the Jordan. Before God took away the latter rains, flocks grazed by the thousands on the mountain sides. From the terraced hill-sides and the valleys the husbandman carried the finest of wheat to Jerusalem. The plains of Esdraelon and Sharon were once gardens of fertility and loveliness. For centuries God withheld the latter rains. Now some rain falls in June, July, and even August, I am told by those who live there. Each year in the last decade this rainfall increases.

The Jews who come to Palestine are not Christians. But has not God said, "I will cleanse them from all their iniquity?" We firmly believe that the time is not far distant when the kingdom shall be restored to Israel and Israel to the kingdom. Then "they shall teach no more every man his neighbor, and every man his brother, saying, Know the Lord: for they shall know me, from the least of them unto the greatest of them, saith the Lord." How God will bring about this great change, we, in our short and imperfect vision, can not fully discern; but the conversion of this people is as sure as his promises.

God has kept the Jews a peculiar people in all the years which have elapsed since they crucified his Son. Although they have been dispersed to every quarter of the globe, they are likewise among the aristocracy of every land. They are to-day among the erudites of the world. They have to this day their hands in the largest manufactories, and control to a great extent the money market of the world. Think you that God will not overrule all this to the glory of that Son they once despised? Will not 'ere long their talents and their wealth be used in the interests of the Cross?

CHAPTER XVIII.

Leprosy—Where seen—Cries—Story of E. Daughan—Ancient mode of treating Lepers—Modern Leper Home—Aim of Fritz Müller—Cause—Contagion.

EVERY visitor to the holy city is familiar with the sad, hoarse cry of the leper. Even before he gets to Jerusalem he is apt to see these poor creatures, and hear their continuous wail of "*Leprous, Hawwafee, Muskeeno, Backshish*"—"I am a leper, gentlemen. I am poor. A present." If he visits the "Tower of the Forty Martyrs," just outside of Ramleh, he can nearly always see a small company of these outcasts amid the ruins. They have no other home. They have been expelled from the village, to subsist upon what they can beg or gather in the fields. Outside of the Leper Home at Jerusalem, I have seen groups of lepers sitting around a kettle, in which they boiled, for their amusement more than to gratify their appetites, grass and herbs which they had gathered from the plain around the Home. The superintendent of the hospital told me that they are so in the habit of this that it now is a source of pleasure; but before they entered the Home it was a necessity.

At Jerusalem there are three places where the lepers principally congregate. The largest crowd is to be seen on the road from Jerusalem to Bethany, just outside of the Garden of Gethsemane, and where the road leads from the main thoroughfare to the "Virgin's Tomb." There is another rendezvous near the Pool of Siloam, and still another near the Jaffa Gate, on the road to Bethlehem.

As soon as they see the traveler approach they set up the most piteous cries. They generally sit by the road-side, in the hot broiling sun. If the passer by pays no attention to them they will gather their ragged garments about them and approach, exhibiting their diseased parts. The sight of these miserable creatures is indelibly fixed on my mind. I can see them yet. Some of them had great horrid spots in their faces. The nose, or the cheek, or chin of some was entirely gone. Others hobbled along on crutches—a limb gone or so diseased that it was useless. Some of them were barefooted, their toes partly gone, and some had their feet tied up in rags.

Of all diseases leprosy is the most loathsome. The bones and the very marrow are pervaded by the awful malady. The members of the body literally fall off, and the patient may well be called a "walking tomb."

The Mosaic law concerning the disease was very rigid. The leper was excluded from the camp, and consequently from the tabernacle. The person was dead to the State and the family when once the priest pronounced the disease leprosy. Even kings were dethroned and shut out from society when it was found that this dread disease had begun its ravages.

This exclusion is still observed in Eastern countries. Elias Daughan, an Arabian evangelist, relates a touching anecdote concerning two leprous boys, which I subjoin in his own words:

"In the first half of June, two leprous boys, about ten or twelve years old, appeared one morning at the asylum and begged to be admitted. They had traveled the night through on foot from Ramleh (30 miles away). It was very touching to see these innocent youths attacked at the very entrance of life by the dread, destructive disease. Still more touching was the story of their short lives. Mr. Müller asked the first about his parents, and whether they had given their assent to his reception into the asylum. Crying pitifully, he answered, amid sobs, that his father had recently died, and his mother had mercilessly turned him out of the house and driven him away from his brothers and sisters. He now has no home; no one cares for him, no man's house and no man's heart stand open to him. The second was calmer, from longer experience of similarly heartless desertion. "My parents," said he, "drove me out of the house more than two years ago, and since then they have troubled themselves no more about me."*

In ancient times leper villages were located outside of the city gates, and in districts away from the main thoroughfares. In the East some of these villages are still in existence. Here the wretched creatures dragged out their miserable existence amidst surroundings and sufferings indescribable. The spiritual life was impure as the physical was diseased. Hospitals for their relief seem to have been unknown in ancient times. In the first years of the Christian era the Church endeavored to follow in the footsteps of the Master. Gregory Nazianzen speaks of a hospital at Cæsarea.

Even in the middle ages, when superstition put

---

*Eighteenth Report of Leper Home, 1889, p. 11.

out the light of holy love in human hearts, the leper was not forgotten. In Jerusalem there was a female Order called St. Lazarus. This Order did much for the victims of the awful disease. After this Order ceased its work, lepers were left to their own devices and to gifts sent them by friends, which at most were few.

In our day there are asylums and hospitals wherever the disease has found a home. Up amidst the ice and snow of Norway, down under the burning suns of Africa, and in far-away India, Christian men and women are spending and being spent for the amelioration of the woes of the leper. But it is of Jerusalem lepers I am writing, and therefore I must speak of what is being done for them there.

I well remember the first time I visited the Leper Home, north of the road to Bethlehem and about a mile from Jerusalem. I had a letter of introduction to the superintendent, Mr. Fritz Müller, given me by a friend in my own city. I was anxious to know how he would receive me. But I had no sooner presented myself than I was conscious that I had found a new friend. Such disinterested friendship as Mr. Müller showed me during my stay of three weeks in Jerusalem I had never before seen. A number of times I went through the large building from cellar to housetop. In my visits I could not help but contrast the cleanliness and comparative contentment of the lepers in this institution with the suffering and despair along the roadside in the places I have mentioned.

Brother Müller and his estimable wife are assisted in their self-denying work by two sisters of. the Moravian church, under whose auspices the hospital was built, and by whose benevolence it is largely supported. These sisters and brothers have literally forsaken all and followed Him whose meat and drink it was to do his Father's will. Every day they cleanse the wounds of the patients and put fresh bandages around them. Every morning Mr. Müller calls them to the chapel and reads and prays for them. These four people cook the food, wash, and do all the nursing for the inmates, of whom there are at present only seventeen; but there is room in the building for seventy. It requires great patience, not a little endurance, and much grace, for these refined people to nurse and care for these degraded and awfully afflicted people, and yet one of these sisters said to me, "How I wish I could do more for my Master."

The great aim of Mr. Müller and his assistants is not to cure leprosy, for so far no cure has been effected; but it is to ease the sufferings of the patients, and above all to lead them to Him who did not disregard the leper's cry when He was on earth. In both these respects they have admirably succeeded. The Superintendent in speaking of the death of one of the inmates, says: "We have seen many die in this manner. We rejoice in the assurance that many have died in the faith of Jesus Christ and entered] into the joy of their Lord."

Some who have never seen leprosy suppose that the disease brings with it very little pain. Quite the contrary is true. Whilst the moral faculties are blunted, and the patient in the last stages is somewhat stupid, the sufferings are intense. Nor do these sufferings continue for a few months only. They are generally prolonged through years, increasing in intensity as the disease progresses.

Is leprosy the result of an immoral life? This question is often asked. Mr. Müller says it is not. Leprosy, it is said, does not as a rule make its appearance before the age of fifteen nor after fifty. There are, however, exceptions, as we have already seen. Filth, uncleanliness of every description, greatly foster the disease.

It is likewise an open question whether leprosy is contagious. It is unquestionably hereditary. Of all the Moravians who have worked among lepers, not one has ever taken the disease. After the First Crusade, leprosy was disseminated through Europe. For many centuries it prevailed to a frightful extent, but it may have been propagated through inheritance and not by contagion. In Palestine it has been known ever since Israel brought it there. It is now confined to the Arabians, with few exceptions. We cannot be too liberal in our gifts to leper hospitals where pious Europeans, and a few natives, literally give their own lives in alleviating the sufferings of the afflicted.

CHAPTER XIX.

Road to Jericho—Bethany—House of Simon the leper—Tomb of Lazarus—Arab guide—Road, dangers of—View—Arab road makers—"Apostles' Fountain"—Lunch—Dangers—View—Monastery—Brook Cherith—Modern Jericho and Jericho of Herod—Kahn—Ride to Dead Sea—On its Shores—Drift-wood—Life—Cities of the Plain—The ride to the Jordan—The river—Pilgrims—Bathing—The return ride—Gilgal—Ancient Jericho—Ruins—Mount of Temptation—Monastery—Reflections.

AS long as I live I will remember the most wonderful ride I took in Palestine. The morning was bright and clear, within a day of the vernal equinox. After selecting a horse from among the twenty which were fastened along the stone wall in front of the "Jerusalem Hotel," we started. There were a dozen tourists and as many dragomen and servants. We formed quite a cavalcade as we wound along the road down to the walls of Jerusalem. We went along the northern wall of the city, taking the road which beyond the northern extremity of Jerusalem passes over the Kedron and along the Garden of Gethsemane. Then it winds toward the east around the foot of Olivet.

In half an hour we were at Bethany, once the home of Mary and Martha and Lazarus.

The house of Simon the leper is still shown on the hillside outside of the village. It is difficult to tell how old the rough stone wall of an ordinary building may be; but we felt quite sure that this ruin was not over ten centuries old. Not far from this ruin is the reputed tomb of Lazarus. After procuring tapers, the traveler descends a distance of about fifteen feet below the level of the street into a chapel or ante-chamber. About ten feet lower is a grotto cut into the solid rock. Inasmuch as "it was a cave" where they laid him, this may have been the very spot where Christ performed the stupendous miracle.

The town of Bethany is in itself small and uninteresting. The houses are low, and of course wholly composed of stones. There are no chimneys on the roofs. When the people have fire, the smoke escapes on the ground through a sort of a conduit opening into the street, or there is no escape or draft except through the door. At Bethany we received our Arab guide. These Arabs, who are all of the Abu Dis tribe, always accompany travelers from Jerusalem to Jericho. They are thieves themselves, but they are paid liberally for their services, and at the end of the trip always demand an additional backsheesh. The road is still infested by thieves, as it was in the days of Christ. This single Arab, with his sword by his side, is the insignia of safety.

A little beyond Bethany the traveler has a fine view of the road he is about to go, as it winds over hill and dale. The Romans constructed most of the road, which was never wide enough for a chariot. No carriages have thus far gone to Jericho. They are at present building a new and good road. I saw men, women and children at work on the road. The people come here from the villages and work out their taxes. These people were half naked, and had very few tools. They carried the dirt in round baskets. For shovels they used their hands largely, or a small narrow affair no better than the hand. Parties numbering ten and twenty had no more than a single mattock with which to cut the earth. Here and there a man with fuse, drill and powder, could be seen at work. These men were evidently imported from some other place. I do not know how long the government has been at work on this road, nor do I know when it will be completed at the present rate of working.

Half an hour's ride from Bethany the traveler

comes to the "Apostles' Fountain," a strong spring issuing from the eastern side of a high hill. This was a landmark between Judah and Benjamin twenty-five centuries ago. I thought we would surely water our horses here, but the dragoman forbade it, saying they had been watered in the early morning, and would travel better without water. The poor beasts traveled all day through the hot sun without food or drink. The Palestine horse is small, sure-footed, and very tough.

We took our dinner of cold chicken, hard-boiled eggs, cold mutton, oranges and bread at the traditional site of the "inn by the way-side," where the good Samaritan left the man who had fallen among thieves. There are two small squares enclosed by stone walls. In these squares the travelers have their luncheon in the shadow of the walls. These, and a high rock at one end of the square, on the right-hand side of the road, afford the only shelter from the heat. There is no tree to be seen in this great barren waste.

We are now at the most dangerous part of our road. I could not be induced for any sum to go over this road alone. Not only was it dangerous in the days of Christ ; but ever since it has borne a hard name. St. Jerome calls it "the bloody way."

A deep ravine beyond the khans is still known as "Murderer's Glen." It was here, only a few years ago, that a gentleman from Baltimore, Md., was robbed.

From this point the road leads through the wildest and grandest scenery in Palestine. You go through narrow gorges, and around high cliffs, and along the edge of frightful precipices. You let the reins hang on your horse's neck, and permit him to pick his own way. Coming around a certain curve of the path, which has here been widened into a broad road, one of the finest views in the Holy Land greets the eye. Spread out before the traveler is the Jordan Valley, now largely an arid waste, but once a veritable garden of fertility. At the lower end of the valley is the Dead Sea, veiled in a sleepy haze, partially hiding the deep green waters. Beyond are the mountains of Moab in stately grandeur, overlooking the blasted plain. To the left, one sees the site of ancient Jericho, and .a little below, the modern village nestling amid the only palms and shrubbery in all the plain. Near the place where we stand, Achan was stoned to death. Through the deep gorge, right below us, and to our left, the brook Cherith once flowed. There is a monastery cut into the solid rock up at the head of the gorge. On the morning of our return we saw many pilgrims wending their way along the narrow path which leads to the plain of Jericho. These people had spent the night in the rocky fastnesses of the monastery, and were now on their way to the Jordan. Most of them had come from Russia, and had literally walked hundreds of miles with their bundles on their backs, and their staves in their hands.

In the rainy season the brook Cherith still asserts its ancient power. The water from the bare hillsides accumulates rapidly in the deep ravine, and comes down the gorge with the noise of thunder, sweeping everything before it. A few days after our ride some of our party tented near the end of the gorge, and came near being washed out of their quarters. I do not wonder that Elijah could safely hide from the wicked Ahab in this gorge.

With this magnificent view we had forgotten that we were tired and very warm from riding in the hot sun for eight long hours. We now descended rapidly into the valley, and were soon upon the site of that Jericho which Christ used to visit. This Jericho is south of the ancient city, about a mile, and consists of the remains of an old Roman aqueduct and |a few stone piles. A ruin, purporting to have been the house of Zacchaeus, is also to be seen. Jericho was once the centre of trade between Arabia and Palestine. It was a strongly fortified city in the days of Ahab. Here was the seat of a school of the prophets which was frequently visited by Elijah. Mark Antony presented the place to Cleopatra, and she, in turn, sold it to Herod. Here this king established his winter residence, it being the most healthy and beautiful spot in his dominions. Jericho was greatly beautified by Herod the Great. Under Vespasian it was destroyed, and afterwards again rebuilt. It was completely destroyed by the Crusaders.

A little before sunset we rode into a khan kept by two Russian ladies. The evening was beautiful; the air was soft and balmy and richly perfumed by orange trees and flowers with which the stone building is surrounded. The gardens here, as in Egypt, are irrigated. There is actually a small spring quite close to the khan at which we stopped. In the days when Lot lived in this valley there was no lack of water, and the land was a veritable garden of the Lord. The half dozen springs which are still in this vicinity could even now be made to irrigate the vale and make it fer-

THE DEAD SEA.

tile; but the people of the place are lazy vagabonds, who would much rather steal than work, whilst the Bedouins who roam here are the most degraded of all the sons of Ishmael. We were very tired, and so retired early. We had learned a lesson by our leaving Jerusalem so late in the morning; we therefore resolved to get an early start for the Dead Sea and the Jordan.

Long before the sun rose we were up and ready for our ride to the Dead Sea. After riding a few miles we came into full view of the sea. There it lay, a great mass of liquid blue! We felt sure it could not be more than a mile to its shore. After riding five miles more we were still a mile away, and apparently no nearer than when we took our first full view. The air is so pure and there are so few small objects that one has very false ideas of distances.

At last we were on the much-wished-for shore. We bathed, picked small stones from beneath the waters, and thoroughly enjoyed our visit to that strange water of which we had heard and read so much in our childhood. The Dead Sea is a remarkable body of water. It is 1300 feet below the level of the ocean, and covers an area of about 300 square miles. It seems as if the bottom were slowly falling out and the waters gradually becoming deeper. Storms frequently lash the heavy waters into fury so that the waves dash high upon the shore. There is no vegetation on its shore. The sands for miles are encrusted with salt which looks like flakes of snow. Here and there were masses of driftwood which comes from one scarcely knows where, up the Jordan or from the mountains of Moab, brought here by the accumulated waters in the ravines in the rainy season. Tristram says, "It is difficult to conceive whence such vast numbers of palms can have been brought, unless we imagine them to be collected wrecks of many centuries, accumulating here from the days when the city of palm trees extended its grove to the edge of the river." The shores of the sea were very quiet when we were there. Frequently, however, birds of many kinds may be seen along the shore. Wild ducks have been observed on the briny waters a mile from the shore. The Sea itself is destitute of all life.

This is not the valley of death it has been described to be. Wild beasts, such as the jackal, hyæna, fox, hare, porcupine, and even the leopard, are seen. At night when the sea is ruffled by the wind it presents great phosphorescent waves, which illuminate its entire surface, and make it a veritable "lake of fire."

It has been asserted that the Cities of the Plain lie buried beneath these waters. It is now generally suppposed that Sodom was situated south of the sea, at what is known as Jebel Usdum. At a place called Gumran, near the northern end of the sea, some remarkable ruins have recently been found. From the similarity of the name, which is supposed to have been preseved by the Arabs, it is asserted that these ruins were once a part of Gomorrah. A large number of graves have been found near here. These graves have vaults at the bottom, built of sun-dried bricks. The bodies found in these tombs all lie with their heads toward the south. They are, therefore, neither Jewish, Mohammedan nor Christian. Outside of what we have in the Bible, little can be known of these wicked cities. The hand of time has wiped out what the wrath of God permitted to remain after that awful morning when Lot went out of Sodom.

The sun even in March burns fiercely in this plain, which is 1300 feet below the level of the sea. The thermometer has been known to register 110° after sunset in July at Engedi, a place on the west side, about half way between the northern and southern ends of the sea.

After leaving the Dead Sea to our right, we rode straight for the Jordan. The Arabs and dragomen of the company gave us fine displays of their excellent horsemanship on the great sandy plain. They rode like madmen, shouting and firing their pistols. Their horses seemed to enjoy it as well as the riders. I had difficulty in restraining my ugly beast from indulging in the same mad sport. I did ride more rapidly than I had done for years at home.

On our nearer approach to the Jordan we began to ride through high dry grass and cane-brakes. We gained our first sight of the historic river a few miles above the spot where it enters the sea, near the place where it is said the children of Israel crossed it when they first entered the plains of Jericho. The bank of the river here was dotted with tents. Garments of every description were drying on bushes. Pilgrims come hither from everywhere, but especially from Russia. Some of them spend a whole week bathing in the historic river and resting from their long and wearisome tramp. Many bathe in a long garment, which they dry and then carefully put away, to serve them as a shroud. They think by bathing their sins are washed away.

THE JORDAN.

Page 264

We encamped at the traditional crossing-place of the children of Israel. We had scarcely dismounted before we were joined by a large party of Cook's tourists, some of whom (among them Drs. Billheimer and Fry of Reading) were known to us. Here we had lunch, and tried to rest in the shade of the trees and shrubs, which at this place are very thick. There were nasty flies which tormented us. In addition it was very hot, there being scarcely a breath of air. The river is very swift and deep here; but, notwithstanding, the greater part of our party took a bath. Many of us took water from the river with us.

The Jordan is a historic river, having been three times miraculously divided. It takes its source in the Springs of Hasbeiya and falls over three thousand feet in its course. It is from 45 to 180 feet wide, and from 3 to 12 feet in depth. There are the remains of several bridges which once crossed the river. Some of these date back to the time of the Romans. There is a fine stone bridge above the site of ancient Jericho.

On our return to Jericho we had a very hot ride. One of our ladies was overcome by the heat and compelled to rest beneath a tree, a few of which dot the plain. We passed a Bedouin camp and saw a slave in the garb bestowed by Dame Nature. These are the hardest looking people I ever saw anywhere.

The return ride was interesting, inasmuch as we passed the traditional site of Gilgal, the first place where the Israelites incamped after their arrival in this plain. The spot where the memorial stones were erected is marked by a large tamarisk-tree. Some claim that the many little mounds scattered around here are none other than the ash-heaps of the children of Israel, produced during that famous encampment of thirty centuries ago!

If this be the place, it is a hallowed spot. Here the male children which had been born during the journey of forty years were circumcised. Flint knives found here seem to confirm the supposition that this was Gilgal and that the knives were used in the performance of the rite. It was here that manna ceased, and it was here that Joshua pitched the tabernacle for the first time in the land of promise. From this encampment the children of Israel marched out every morning for seven days to encompass the city which once stood a few miles to the north of Gilgal.

Of coure we went to the site of old Jericho. The fountain which gushes from a hillock which may be partly composed of the ruined wall of the ancient City of Palms, is, no doubt, the very spring whose bitter waters Elisha healed. The hillocks, which are seen in different places near the fountain, are nearly all artificial. Some of these hillocks are of stone within or of sun-dried bricks. They were used either for defence or for the purpose of locating altars dedicated to idols. This is the spot where God gave one of the grandest manifestations of His power to help His people. In this city was Rahab's house who secreted the spies, and who, in the wonderful providence of God, became the mother of a line of illustrious ancestors,* whose glory culminated in the Messiah. That she was a harlot in the modern sense of the word is no necessary conclusion, inasmuch as she, no doubt, kept an inn and in consequence was called a harlot.

If the fountain of Elisha were kept clean, its waters would be delicious. Wherever its healing waters flow there is an abundance of vegetation. If the water were properly conducted it could be made to irrigate the whole plain for miles around, and restore to it something of its ancient product-

---

* Rahab married a prince in Judah, became the mother of Boaz, who married Ruth, who was the ancestor of David, through whom the Messiah came.

iveness. One can not help asking whether in the infinite wisdom of the Father this plain is not held in desolation until all nations shall have come to the Son, then to be restored to its ancient glory in the last days, when the Master reigns on earth in the hearts of all people. Directly back of ancient Jericho rises one of the highest mountains of the Judean range. This mountain has been pointed to for many centuries as the scene of Christ's temptation and forty days' fast. On the top of the mountain are the ruins of a Christian church dating back to the days of the Crusaders. Up there veiled in clouds these brave men used to worship God. What wonder if they and the monks in their rock-hewn cells had views grander than that which Moses had from Nebo yonder. The mountain is literally honeycombed with cells once the homes of monks. Many of these are almost inaccessible. The rains and storms of centuries have left frightful precipices where once men could walk with ease. From our hostelry we could see lights twinkle in these airy fastnesses. When all these cells were inhabited as they once were, it is said lights burned nightly in every rock-hewn home, illuminating the entire mountain side. Just when these wonderful homes were first occupied is not so easy to determine. Many suppose that the early Christians went thither to escape bloody persecutions. Others followed them from choice. It is said those who live there now obtain all their provisions from Jerusalem, to which some of their number walk daily. I wonder whether they always depended upon this source for their supplies, or whether they were at times fed by angels or ravens, as was Elijah, not many miles from this mountain?

As the evening shadows were lengthening I stood above old Jericho, and looked on the peaceful, naked plain below. There was Gilgal and the Jericho of Herod. Beyond these the smoke of a few Bedouin camp-fires ascended, as the smoke of incense used to ascend from the Tabernacle of God's people. Still further the waters of the Dead Sea lay quiet as a child in dreamless slumber. To the left the Jordan rushed wildly in its zigzag course, as if in conscious haste to bury itself in its strange sea tomb.

Then I saw this plain thickly covered with trees and gardens and homes. I saw a great company coming like a great cloud from beyond the Jordan. I fancied I heard their songs of triumph as they pitched their tents at Gilgal. Again the scene changed, and I saw half a score of chariots driven to the historic river. I saw Naaman, the leper, bathe where Israel had crossed; I saw him healed from his awful malady. Again my mind bounded over the deep chasm of the years, and I heard the voice of John calling sinners to repentance on those historic banks. I heard the "Man of Sorrows" say, "Suffer it to be so now, for thus it becometh us to fulfil all righteousness." I felt that I had not come in vain to this now desolate place; this place where heaven had so often come down to earth in mercy as well as judgment. In this small district of country Faith has won some of its grandest victories, and Sin has found its most awful punishment. The eye can not look anywhere here without resting upon some spot sacred because of its associations with Old and New Testament saints. Do you wonder, therefore, kind reader, that I have said |that I will never, so long as I live, forget my visit to Jericho, the Jordan and the Dead Sea?

CHAPTER XX.

Hebron—Road and associations—Field of Boaz—Episode—Bethlehem—Church of the Nativity—St. Jerome—Plain of the Shepherds—"Wells of David"—Memories—The People and Industries—Tomb of Rachel—Giloh—"Pool of Solomon"—Aqueduct—Gardens—Cave of Adullam—Amos—Resting place—"Oak of Abraham"—View—Hebron—Age—Cave of Machpelah—Return to Jerusalem.

THE road from Jerusalem to Hebron is probably the oldest and one of the most interesting in Palestine. Parts of this road were in use already in the days of Abraham. Upon the Plain of Rephaim David twice encountered the Philistines, and, no doubt, crossed and recrossed this road. In this vicinity the sweet singer of Israel was hunted by Saul like a wild beast. Along this highway he afterwards went in triumph the crowned king of Israel, from Hebron to take up his royal residence in Jerusalem. The Man of Sorrows himself was carried, and, no doubt, afterwards trod this very road from the home of his birth to the Holy City. The road is intimately associated with the life of patriarchs and prophets, kings and counsellors, inasmuch as Hebron from the earliest days of Israel's history was an important place.

We left our hotel at 5 o'clock, before the sun had ascended the dark mountains of Moab. When his first rays lit up the hills we were already beyond the German colony and well across the Plain of Rephaim.

The finest and largest modern building which the tourist passes in his entire journey from Jerusalem to Hebron is the Leper Hospital under the auspices of the Moravian church. We have already spoken of this truly beautiful and comfortable home in a previous chapter. We soon come to the fields in which the youthful widow, Ruth, once gleaned after the reapers in the fields of Boaz. This was more than 3000 years ago, but the story of her life so graphically related in the Book of Ruth will live forever. We are soon in sight of Bethlehem, the birthplace of the Bread of Life. Here we had quite an episode, which I must relate. Four tourists and two dragomen, together with the driver, occupied one of the three lumbering wagons which had been engaged for our journey. I had noticed that the two dragomen and the driver were engaged in quite an animated conversation in Arabic for some time. I said, "What is up?" The dragoman said, "He (the driver) says, he will not go to Hebron." The very journey for which he had been engaged he now refused to make. Soon the driver stopped the vehicle. The dragomen started the horses and the conversation became more animated. Then of a sudden the dragomen gave the driver a couple smart thumps and threw him off his own wagon, and we drove on. I told the dragomen he would have us all arrested at Hebron. But Ephraim, our older dragoman, said, "He is only a Jew. If he says one word I'll have *him* arrested." In the evening when we came to the place where the fight occurred, Mr. Jew made profuse apologies and remounted as if nothing had occurred. There was a time, not so long ago, in which a Jew was not tolerated in the city of Jerusalem. If a Turk or an infidel met a Jew he could compel him to carry burdens for miles, and reward him at the end of the journey with a blow.

The day was already far spent when we entered Bethlehem. We visited Bethlehem on the way *from* Hebron, but I will here narrate briefly what I saw in this sacred city. Of course everybody on entering Bethlehem goes to the Church of the Nativity. This church was built by the Empress Helena, and is the oldest Christian church in the world. It is richly adorned with columns, and gold and silver lamps. The cedar roof rests upon forty-eight beautiful columns, which no doubt once occupied a place in the Temple of Solomon. That the grotto in this church, which purports to be the very one in which Christ was born, is the identical spot of our Saviour's nativity, there is no need to doubt. Not only is this the spot to which tradition has pointed for eighteen hundred years, but Justin Martyr, who was born in Syria, and who had every opportunity to know the place, points to this cave as the one in which Christ was born. Helena must have felt quite certain of the place before she erected her grand basilica. This magnificent church has a nave and double aisles. The aisles are separated by a double row of monolithic columns, ornamented with Corinthian capitals. Passing through the church, the visitor descends thirteen steps to the crypt. Here is the Chapel of the Nativity, a cave, the floor and sides of which are covered with beautiful marble. This chapel is thirteen and one half yards long, four yards wide and ten feet high. Under the altar is a silver star in the marble pavement, with the inscription: *Hic de Virgine Maria Jesus Christus natus est* (Here Jesus Christ was born of the Virgin

Mary). The chapel is lighted by thirty-two beautiful lamps, which are said to be kept burning night and day from century to century. About the altar which marks the birthplace of Christ there are fifteen of these lamps. In the Chapel of the Manger Jesus was laid after his birth, and adored by the Magi (Matthew ii. 11). In another place is shown the spot where Joseph slept when he was "warned of God in a dream that they should not return to Herod." St. Jerome for a time lived in Bethlehem. Under his direction monasteries, and a hostelry and hospital for pilgrims, were built here. A little cell cut out of the solid rock, in which St. Jerome used to write and meditate, is still to be seen. Here he translated the Bible into Vulgate, and here he died and was buried. The stone steps which he used to ascend and descend are now in the wall of the Church of the Nativity. In 416 the Pelagians burned his establishment at Bethlehem, and he fled for his life. Two years afterwards he returned, and not long after this his labors ceased. He was buried among the ruins of his monastery. It is said his remains were afterwards exhumed and taken to the Church of Santa Maria Maggiora in Rome.

We ascended the hill from which we could see

the angels stood in holy rapture when Christ was born. It was thither the star came and stood over the place where the young Child lay, that Child whose "line is gone out through all the earth, and His words to the end of the world." What forces that birth has started against the powers of darkness! What holy aspirations His life has kindled! What hopes it has awakened! Bethlehem here, and the Cross on Calvary yonder, are the two spots from which the history of humanity takes a new start, and to which it points for the origin of the new and the grand development of these latter days.

Bethlehem is still the garden spot for many miles around Jerusalem. The hills are terraced and the limestone rocks with which they are studded are covered with olive orchards, choice vines, and clustering figs. Its people are the prettiest, the tallest and most intelligent, we met anywhere in all this wonderful land. The people manufacture the finest articles out of mother of pearl made anywhere. These goods make beautiful and useful souvenirs, and are remarkably cheap when we consider the time and skill required in their making.

About six miles from Jerusalem the traveler

comes to a small structure apparently of modern date. This spot has been looked upon for many centuries as the Tomb of Rachel, the beloved wife of Jacob. We are told that her husband buried her, "in the way of Ephrath, which is Bethlehem. And Jacob set a pillar upon her grave: that is the pillar of Rachel's grave unto this day." Leah, her sister, sleeps in the cave of Machpelah; but the ashes of Rachel have reposed here alone through all the centuries. As one gazes upon the old tombs of Bible characters, and walks over the hills and valleys through which they once roamed, one becomes strangely familiar with their hallowed lives and more deeply interested in the Book which records God's dealings with them.

As the traveler continues his journey he comes to Giloh, the old home of Ahithophel, the friend and counselor of David. This friend the king lost in his old age when he was compelled to flee from Absalom. Beyond Giloh are the Pools of Solomon. There is little doubt that the construction of these reservoirs dates back to the time of Israel's wisest king. Traces are to be seen of five broken aqueducts from ten to thirty miles long, entering Jerusalem from the south. Three of these connect with the Pools. There are three of these Pools, measuring in all 1385 feet in length, and 236 in width. Their depth is from twenty-five to forty feet. They are in successive terraces one below the other, and about fifty yards apart. The water was gathered from springs, some of them miles away. The conduits leading from the springs to the pools were concealed, so that an enemy could not not cut off the supply. One of these conduits is four miles long. One of the aqueducts follows the modern plan of piping, showing that Jewish artisans were familiar with the principles applied in the construction of reservoirs and the conveying of water supplies in modern times. Instead of using iron or wooden piping, they used large blocks of stone neatly joined. Through the centre of these blocks they bored or drilled a hole sixteen inches in diameter. The whole tube is imbedded in rubble-work and coated with cement. It is said Solomon's gardens were here close to these Pools. Here he planted vineyards and olive orchards, fruits and flowers. To this place he is said to have driven in his chariot every morning. Here he sought peace from the cares of state, and satisfaction for his burdened soul, but found it not. Of all these things he wrote, "Vanity of vanities!" "All is vanity and vexation of spirit."

Not far from the Pools of Solomon is a cleft in the rock where Samson is said to have hid himself from the Philistines after smiting them "hip and thigh" for burning his wife and her family. (Judges xv. 1).

The cave of Adullam, in which David took refuge when he fled from the king of Gath, is also not far from the Pools. David knew every inch of ground in this vicinity, for it was upon these hills he kept his father's flocks before he exchanged the shepherd's crook for the diadem of Israel. "The cave is in the north face of a precipitous mountain, and the only approach is along a narrow, shelving rock, overhanging the dry bed of a stream a hundred feet below." The entrance is narrow, but the cave itself is large, consisting of galleries, rooms and halls. Every foot of the ground in this vicinity is sacred, having been trodden and re-trodden by prophet, priest and king. The home of Amos, and that of the woman who interceded for Absalom with David, his father, was also in this vicinity. (2 Sam. xiv. 1-20.)

About five miles beyond the Pools of Solomon we stopped at a hut by the wayside, near a spring.

ABRAHAM'S OAK.

In this hut they furnish coffee and horse-feed to the hundreds of pilgrims who pass this way every year, to and from Hebron. After a short rest, we were off once more. In about two hours we were opposite the Hotel Hebron, where we dismissed our horses, and went up a by-way about a mile to the oak on the plain of Mamre.

The "Oak of Abraham," as it is called, is a large tree more than twenty feet in circumference. It is now held together with chains, and the decayed places in the trunk are filled with putty. Notwithstanding this great care, it will not be long before the storms, which it has withstood for centuries, will prostrate it. We took luncheon under this old tree, and brought away with us some of its acorns. This is not the oak under which Abraham and Sarah pitched their tent four thousand years ago; but it is near, if it does not overshadow the spot. After luncheon we ascended the tower on the top of the hill behind the oak, and had a splendid view of the Dead Sea on our right, and the mists which overhung the blue Mediterranean on our left. This view is almost as fine as the one from the top of Olivet.

Having no other means, inasmuch as we had dismissed our carriages, we walked to the town, nearly two miles away. Hebron is the oldest town in the world. It "was built seven years before Zoan in Egypt." The very site of the latter is in dispute, whilst Hebron is as thriving and prosperous as any town in modern Palestine. We marvel at the antiquities of ruined Memphis; but Hebron was old before the foundations of Memphis were laid. The oldest relics of Roman civilization are recent when compared with Hebron. It was built long before Joseph was sold to the Ishmaelites, or before the first verse of the Bible was written. Near this town Abraham entertained his heavenly visitors. Years afterwards, when Abraham was with the angels, and his children had escaped their bondage and were returning to this very land, the spies bore back in triumph to the assembled hosts the fruits of this land. When Israel was established in this land centuries afterwards, his second, and in many respects his greatest king, began his reign in Hebron.

The cave of Machpelah which Abraham purchased from Ephron, the Hittite, for four hundred shekels of silver, is in Hebron. This burial place is covered by a mosque, which is held in the greatest reverence by the fanatical Mohammedans. Well they may reverence this ancient burial place, for of all the sacred places in their unhallowed possession few are more worthy of reverence. Here Sarah was buried. In due time Abraham was laid here. Then came the ashes of an illustrious line of Jewish ancestors for many ages. No doubt the ashes of Jacob were brought thither from from Egypt. The "Haram and Castle of Abraham," as the sacred enclosure is called, contains at the southern end what was once a Christian church. This doubtless covers a tomb which contains the ashes of the patriarchs. It is said there are two caves, one above the other. In the lower are the ashes of the patriarchs, and in the upper many human bones brought there centuries ago to await the resurrection near the great ancestor of this wonderful people. We were not in the mosque. Christians are not admitted. The Prince of Wales and a few others are the only Christians that have been in the sacred enclosure since the religion of the False Prophet has had the land in its power. When will the time come when Palestine and all its sacred treasures will be in the possession of Christian nations, to whom alone they belong? Before this comes to pass, the millenium of Christ's reign can not come.

After leaving Hebron we returned to Jerusalem,

which to every pilgrim is the great centre of attraction. From the Holy City all of our short excursions to the towns and places of interest were made. Our return ride was as pleasant as any we had in Palestine. We met and passed many pilgrims on their way to and from Hebron. This city is of like interest to Christian, Jew and Mohammedan, inasmuch as all claim its sacred relics.

DAMASCUS.

Page 285

CHAPTER XXI.*

Damascus — Description — History — Paul in Damascus — Bazaars—Rugs—Silks—Blades—Great Mosque—John of Damascus, Tomb of—Of Saladin—Private houses—Christian missions.

DAMASCUS! The traveler looks back to it with a pleasure which no memory of its dirt and dogs can destroy. The approach to the city keeps a party quiet. It is all so beautiful. The river Abana, which Naaman thought better than the Jordan, (and no wonder!) flows through it, and the verdure is specially thick and delightful after that long, hot ride up the country. The houses are generally white, with enough of the darker shades to bring out the minarets and towers more distinctly. The city appears first as a long white line against the blue, punctuated with these shapely spires, and as one gets nearer it gains in beauty. The road winds along the hill-side (a spur of the Lebanons), and gives a fine view of the city; then goes down through the famous gardens, and enters the city

---

*I am indebted to Rev. Prof. C. B. McAfee of Park College for this and following chapter.

on the smooth carriage road from Beirut. What a history the city has had! Naaman was here, and the conductor dutifully points out the site of his residence, which is now appropriately occupied by a hospital for lepers. Long after, the city figures in prophecy for condemnation. Then Saul came to it, and went out Paul. The house of Ananias is shown, and that of Judas, where Saul was taken, and where Ananias found him. The latter is fitted up with candles, an altar, and the necessaries for worship. It will always be inseparably connected with whitewash in my mind, because it had just been whitened, and had not a pleasant odor. So easy is it to go from the sublime to the ridiculous.

Paul escaped from Damascus by a basket over the wall, you remember. The place is pointed out, and is, within the range of possibility, the correct one. Some people are skeptical enough to shake their heads and doubt it, but such people have much to doubt in Palestine.

There were Jewish synagogues here in Christ's time, and in the time of Constantine it became the seat of a Christian patriarch, whose authority ranked next to that of Antioch. A very large Christian Church was here. Persecuting Paul did not stop his work.

In the seventh century after Christ the Mohammedans took the city, and have held it with very slight intermissions ever since. Saladin made it his headquarters for a time, and the Turks got it in the sixteenth century. So much for history.

The bazaars of Damascus are one of the great attractions. The three specialties are rugs, silks and blades. Besides these there are whole rows of shops, whose fronts are decorated with red and yellow shoes, or with toys, fruit, harness, mats, and what not. A large part of the "Street called Straight," is now shops of all sorts. Several of the streets are roofed with high arches, and thus the fine arcades of Milan and Florence are replaced. The merchants of Damascus are of the usual Oriental sort. They ask twice what they hope to get. A fez starts at three francs (60 cents), and you get it easily enough for one franc; a rug is priced at $30 and sold for $20. The buyer does not expect the seller to tell him the truth about the goods, so the seller does not try to tell it. Once in a long while a dealer is found who means what he says, and will not come down in price, but it is not often. I found one, and was so surprised that I bought something I did not want. Many tourists buy Damascus rugs as souvenirs. They are beautiful, and can be had at any price. They would be called expensive were they not so serviceable and lasting ; $25 will not buy a very large one, $10 will get a small one. I saw one for $350, but it was enormous and heavy. There is certainly a large choice. Even the small dealers seem to have an unlimited supply, and to be proud of them, even though they sell none.

The silks are equally beautiful. It seemed to me the colors were brighter and clearer than anywhere else. Red, yellow and green impressed me as the most common colors, though blue and other tints were to be seen. Some of the patterns were delicate and really fine ; others were of the most impossible design and looked gaudy.

Damascus steel blades are justly famous. They are of all shapes and sizes, from the little hunter's knife to the belt sword of the sheik. Showing us the quality of these latter, the dealer cut a nail almost in two with it, and I looked in vain for the damage to the blade! They gain in value if they have been used, and so it is almost impossible to find one which has not been owned by some great cut-throat. A merchant assured me in broken English that a blade which I was examining had killed more men than he or I had. I assured him that so far as I was concerned, that said nothing for the blade, since I kept no private graveyard. Then I asked him how many fellow-men had fallen beneath his vengeance. His English was exhausted, so he said, "Yes," and I felt unanswered. But I did not buy the blade.

It would be impossible to describe the bazaars except at great length. Generally goods of the same kind may be found together. There will be a whole row of fez shops, and then shoes, and then veils, and then rugs, and so on. Once in a while a dealer carries more than one line, but as a rule he has room for very little, and keeps one line only.

The sights of the city are not very abundant. Chief among them is the Great Mosque, with its two slender minarets, its tomb of John of Damascus, and its relics of the early Christian Church. The latter consist of two bronze doors, and a Greek inscription over a doorway long since blocked up. The inscription is a quotation of Ps. cxlv. 13, and is usually covered with clap-boards, which are removed for a fee. It was of special interest to the clergymen of the party, and was promptly booked as an illustration. It is said that this is the site of the House of Rimmon, of Naaman's time, and also that the great Church was here. At any rate the present Mosque has a great interest. It was so expensive with frescoes and marbles that the Sultan had all the expense-sheets destroyed, lest the people be offended at his prodigality. Only a few traces of its early finery are left, but they hint of costly things. John of Damascus, whose tomb is in the mosque, was a pious theologian of the eighth century. His tomb is a large one, and rather overdone with bronze and glass. As we passed through, a child's body lay before it waiting burial. We saw it carried out presently, and were told that the custom obtains among a great many of the faithful, of leaving the bodies here an hour. The tomb is near the east end of the building.

Not far from it is the famous well, from which if you drink five times a day you become younger all the time. Some of our ladies were observed to take five distinct sips of the water. I do not know if it worked, but there was no need for any such antidote.

The tombs of Saladin and his son are in a building close by, and really under the shadow of the Great Mosque. These tombs are large in themselves and occupy a building whose roof is really worth study as a successful arch. I fear I did not gain much from the tombs, but I brought away an impression of the building as one of striking sympathy and beauty. The fame of Saladin might well rest on the fact that his word was never broken. We may be pardoned for having smiled vociferously when some remarked as we came out, "This is the fellow who had such a wonderful lamp that he rubbed, isn't it?"

The panorama of the city seen from the minaret will never be forgotten, and cannot be described. The place of the Druse massacre of 1860 was pointed out. Dozens of minarets, several arched streets, hundreds of curved roofs, and people moving about, left a distinct impression.

Damascus is wealthy. We were told that there are several men worth over half a million, and we visited two houses which betokened immense wealth. One had belonged to a Jew, who loaned the government a large sum ; and the government, with a nonchalance peculiar to the Turks, declined to pay principal or interest, and the poor fellow died of a broken heart after fitting up one room in fabulous fashion. Mirrors and marbles, rich upholstering, divans, inlaid tables—everything was costly ; and there were other houses like it. Just how much the women have to do with it I do not know; but if the presence of one woman brightens a house, as is claimed in America, how bright four ought to make one in Damascus? One place had a court in the center, which was beautiful with trees and a fountain; flowers were profuse, and life was worth living certainly, if anywhere, in Damascus.

Christianity in this old city has not the power it should have. There are missions there, and we attended their services. The natives are being reached, but the work is not being done as rapidly as we could wish. Those who are there are faithful laborers, and have evident divine blessing. There ought to be more of them, however. Mohommedanism is *not* "good enough for the Arabs and Turks," nor for anybody else for that matter. The more Christianity Damascus has the higher it will come. Here, as everywhere, missions are humanitarian as well as divine. The gospel teaches sanitation as well as salvation. It will teach the Damascenes to wash as well as to worship, and that will be a great gain. It may lead them to kill some of their dogs; but that is expecting too much, perhaps.

ATHENS.

CHAPTER XXII.

Athens—Drive to the city—A soldier—Language—Prices—Museums—The Acropolis—The Odeon—Temple of Theseus—Of Jupiter—The Citadel—Gates—The Parthenon—"Unwinged Victory"—Mars' Hill.

WHY does one get excited as he nears the fulfillment of a dream? Why did we hurry on deck that Saturday morning, and look silently across the water and land to see the mountains that lay back of the city, and the ruins that marked the summit of the Acropolis, and the white buildings which were the city? We were nearing Athens. Most of us had lost our sentimentality and effusiveness by the severe shocks of the past weeks, but we could not be unimpressed as the city came more clearly into view. It is not on the seacoast, you remember, but lies five miles inland, with its harbor guarded by Piraeus. This is no small city, of itself. It makes an American shake himself, as though he might be nearer home than the guide-book says. But we did not protest when we were put into carriages and started for Athens. The dust was dreadful, and the intelligent drivers kept at just the right distance from each other for us to catch the clouds as they came down. They were all Greeks, so I have no idea what they were thinking, but I know they were long-visioned gentlemen. We got all the dust there was to get. But we didn't mind that—Athens was only five miles away.

There is a good carriage road all the way over from Piraeus, and the drive did not seem long. We were in full view of the ruins of the Parthenon and the Eurechtheium, though we did not call them by that name then. Mounts Lycabettus and Pentelius made a clear impression. We were not at all weary of seeing, when we got to the hotel.

Athens is modern. Its streets are broad, well paved, and generally well lighted. They abound in marble, and are beautified by well arranged and decorated stores. You might set this city down in our country, and call it an improvement on ours. It has its ragged edges, of course, but so have our cities. Of course the dress is mostly European, but the Greek soldier was a standing curiosity to me. What masculine architect ever devised his outfit, I cannot imagine, and how he has the bravery to wear it is as remarkable. The waist of it is ornamented with some sort of tinsel, and is generally worn tight. The skirt of it is white, and reaches to the knees, enlarging there until your soldier looks baggy, decidedly. Then he is finished off with white stockings, which sometimes fail to connect with the skirt, and a pair of low shoes. I am not sure that this description is lucid beyond what might be expected from a gentleman's observation of such a toilet. Of course, we were on the *qui vive* for the language. The accent and pronunciation seemed wholly different from what we learned when we were in college. The best authority* I could find there sneers at our pronunciation, and declares it was never used in speech—as of course we had supposed. Certainly the rhythm and music of the present language surpass what we made of Homer years ago. English and French are crowding in, however, and within a few decades will begin to restrict the beautiful Greek, I fear. Languages are as imperious as men, and one must give way before another.

There is nothing distinctively Athenian which the tourist can buy, except marbles from one place and another, and shells from Marathon and Sal-

---

*Dr. Kalopothekes, a native missionary.

amis. They do not manufacture things in any abundance, so far as we found, but they are a plucky little nation, bound to succeed. Tourists are welcome, and are treated well. In some cases the price of things is absurdly high. I even heard a lady complaining over the price of some hair pins! I tremble to think what a suit of clothes would have cost there. I bought a knife for about forty cents, knowing it could not be any good. One blade snapped when I attempted to sharpen a pencil therewith. I keep the handle and another blade as a souvenir. In most cases, however, prices are fair and dealers courteous. The people seemed very cordial everywhere we went while there.

Greece is rich in memories, and excavations yield large results. Dr. Schliemann has made a name for himself and a handsome profit for the nation by his enthusiastic work in unearthing ruins. Consequently there are some fine museums.

It is rank heresy, but I confess I was tired of museums. Things get so musty and unreal after they are laid under a glass case, or stood up in a row against a wall. A man who can move about and talk will bear closer acquaintance than a dozen pieces of old crockery and patched statues. The

Athenian museums are fine, but they are museums, and they are interesting, or not, as you like or do not like "antiques." There are ship prows pulled out of the sea, gold cups, tankards, old knives, swords, skeletons, crockery, costumes, and so on. It was worth noting that some of the colors of the frescoes were as bright as though they were fresh. The statues were called fine, but—well, they were fine, I suppose. The museum buildings are very fine, and are evidence of what Greece may become. They are of white marble, and stand out uncrowded, low and massive.

Nothing in Athens compares in interest with the Acropolis. It is a high hill, crowned with ruins of what must have been a magnificent group of buildings. All around one side of the hill, at the base, are ruins. Among the latter are the ruins of the Theatre of Bacchus, with its space for 35,000 people, who endured the stone seats for the sake of the play. Strange to say, the front row of seats in this tragic theatre was reserved for the priests! Imagine it now! There are names engraved on the stone chairs, and it was pleasant to sit where dignity had sat.

Next the theatre is the shrine of Esculapius, which shows the effect of time and tourists. Beside it is the Odeon of Herodes Atticus, a neater little ampitheatre, with enough left to prove that it was worthy the city in its day. It was intended for reciting poetry and such things. I noticed the walls seemed very strong and the entrance easily guarded, presumably to protect the poet from the populace. The Odeon has a seating capacity of about 6,000 we were told. As we sat about resting, it was natural that we should sing "America," and try to forget that we were so far away from there. Most of the front wall of the Odeon stands, and shows how the exits were arranged. In the centre of the pavement, between the platform and the seats, is a cistern, which helped to cool the audience, and when necessary, the declaimers. No one is authority for the statement, but it seems a plain fact.

The reputed prison of Socrates, where he was kept just before he took poison, is worthy only a mention. There are three caverns cut in the rock on a hillside across the valley from the Acropolis. One is square, one circular, one irregular. All are shallow and have iron bars at the entrance. I do not know which is Socrates' prison, and am not sure of either.

Everything about is historic. There is the

bema of the orators. It is a platform cut out of rock. Demosthenes delivered the *Oratio De Corona* here. Standing on it we see the city with Lycabettus for a background. The Acropolis is most conspicuous from here, as it is from everywhere.

The temple of Theseus is between here and the hotel, and is worthy a visit. The road to Corinth must be crossed, and no doubt Paul traveled it. The Theseum is built on a spur, almost on the plain, that runs out from Mars' Hill. It marks the site of the second burial of Theseus. This hero lived 1700 B. C., and was nearly contemporary with the Pentateuch. He introduced a system of government into Attika, and after dying in the usual way, appeared again at the battle of Marathon. This somewhat surprised people, and he took high rank among them as a saint. "I omit the details," as our conductor used to say. The building is not large, is oblong, surrounded of course with a row of columns, unlighted until it was doctored up for a church. It is 2200 years old, we are told. What makes this masonry more remarkable, it is cut to fit so closely that there is no mortar. The roof is modern, and at first the building was open above, then covered and left dark. It is an amateur museum, and has the regulation tablets and refuse in it. The finest parts of all are the tablets which have cut on them the laws of ancient Greece. One would like time to read them through, but cannot. They are in Greek whose letters look familiar in spite of being so old.

On the other side of the Acropolis is the temple of Jupiter, dating from the 6th century B. C. It is all gone but fifteen columns, and they are wonderful. They are high, large, and stand up as lonely sentinels. One has fallen, and lies along the ground with the clean-cut edges of the fluted stones separated. One can see what close fitting has been done. In all these buildings mortar seems to have been unthought of. The masons cut the stones so well that they fitted and stayed there. It is difficult to imagine what this temple of Jupiter must have been, but it was certainly worthy the city and the divinity. The goverment is protecting the ruins as well as it can, but of course some vandals love to carry home pieces of everything, and so the fallen column is all scarred up by the meanness of men.

Not far from this temple is the Stadium, which was the place for foot-races, and other manly sports. And to get to it you must needs cross the "classic Illyssus." This is not much to look at. It is between 3 and 25 inches wide, has a rich green scum on it, and does not seem to be going anywhere. The poetry of history gets more poetic the more facts one learns. The king's palace, the mansion of Dr. Schliemann, the explorer, the churches and many other things, are duly visited by all tourists, but would not be of much interest if described.

Of the two great points of interest in Athens, something must be said. First, the Acropolis. It has been the citadel and fortress of Athens many a time. It is almost unassailable except from one side. No one knows just when it began to be a religious power as well as military. It lies south of the main part of the city, but west of many of the buildings, and is a single point that shoots heavenward, out of the plain. The top is broad enough for many people, and much building, and has been faithfully used by both. The accessible side is the west, and there were the main gates to the summit. A broad stairway led to the five-fold gate, and through them processions entered. The Propylea was of itself a beautiful piece of work, and though very much ruined, still repays careful study. There are five gates side by side. The two outside are smallest and of the same size; the next two are larger, and the central is highest of all. There are marks of the hanging of gates, apparently, and the capstones of the doors are fine specimens of stone. One or two have fallen. Once on the top, the largest ruin is the highest—the Parthenon. It is much like the mental picture we all have of it from its photographs. Neither wall is complete, and several of the columns are thrown down. The west end is most nearly complete. It formerly opened toward the east, and had no door toward the west, but when it was made a church, a door was cut in the west. The site of the great statue which was the glory of the Parthenon can still be traced easily. There is a winding stairway at the west end, which goes up through the wall. It is said by some to have been a Moslem piece of work, and the top used as a minaret. Possibly it was always there. At any rate, I will never forget climbing those steps in the evening of a certain day, and sitting high up on these ruins waiting for the moon to rise, and the beauty of the scene as the moonlight came over it will always be fresh in my mind. The Parthenon is oblong, with two rows of columns at each end, and one row at the sides. It crowns the hill, and deserves to crown it.

This is the largest ruin, but it is not the finest. The best specimen of archæological industry and of original taste is the little temple of Nike Apteros, or Unwinged Victory. It is very small, and stands unconnected with anything, on the very southwest corner of the summit. It had been cast down and the pieces were scattered, but two enthusiasts saw its possibilities and put it together again. Photographs of it and everything else on the Acropolis abound, and will give more of an idea of the ruins than any new description can give.

The other, and to me the most important place in Athens, is a small hill west of the Acropolis. Steps are cut in the stone and they have been trodden by thousands of people, and for hundreds of years. It is Mars' Hill. How many great speeches and strong defences have been made here! Theorists used to come here, and a great many whose theories proved eternal truths. In Paul's time there were more than 2,000 divinities represented in Athens, and yet to-day only one, and He the Unknown God, is worshipped there. Paul seemed presumptuous, his preaching made no impression on the mass of people, but he has all history since to vindicate him. The speech delivered on that knoll was forgotten the next day by the Athenians; but those ruins we have just left, and the church spires down yonder in the city, tell whether it is still forgotten.

There is really nothing to describe about Mars' Hill. It is not so pretty as many a little hill about your home. Its stones are not impressive, its seamed sides are not poetic. Common things cannot be made uncommon by phrases. Simply as a geographical study, Mars' Hill yields no profit. But seen historically Mars' Hill is a mountain. It speaks for the God no longer Unknown, but loved and followed by millions.